TECHNICAL
REPORT

Cold-Case Investigations

An Analysis of Current Practices and Factors Associated with Successful Outcomes

Robert C. Davis, Carl Jensen, Karin E. Kitchens

Sponsored by the National Institute of Justice

RAND Center on Quality Policing

A RAND INFRASTRUCTURE, SAFETY, AND ENVIRONMENT CENTER

This research was sponsored by the National Institute of Justice and was conducted in the RAND Center on Quality Policing within the Safety and Justice Program of RAND Infrastructure, Safety, and Environment.

Library of Congress Cataloging-in-Publication Data

Davis, Robert C. (Robert Carl)
Cold-case investigations : an analysis of current practices and factors associated with successful outcomes / Robert C. Davis, Carl Jensen, Karin E. Kitchens.
p. cm.
Includes bibliographical references and index.
ISBN 978-0-8330-5904-8 (pbk. : alk. paper)
1. Criminal investigation—United States. 2. Forensic sciences—United States. I. Jensen, Carl. II. Kitchens, Karin E. III. Title.

HV8073.D297 2011
363.250973—dc23

2011040178

Published 2011 by the RAND Corporation
1776 Main Street, P.O. Box 2138, Santa Monica, CA 90407-2138
1200 South Hayes Street, Arlington, VA 22202-5050
4570 Fifth Avenue, Suite 600, Pittsburgh, PA 15213-2665
RAND URL: http://www.rand.org/
To order RAND documents or to obtain additional information, contact
Distribution Services: Telephone: (310) 451-7002;
Fax: (310) 451-6915; Email: order@rand.org

Preface

Fueled by the popularity of television shows focusing on forensic investigation, cold-case investigations have captured the imagination of the American public, and cold-case investigations have become increasingly commonplace in law enforcement agencies.[1] Yet, despite the increasing number of cold-case units and the expenditure of significant resources to fund them, we know virtually nothing about the return on this investment. This report seeks to help better understand cold-case investigation, discussing the status of cold-case investigations in the United States and examining factors associated with successful cold-case investigations. The research was funded by the National Institute of Justice (NIJ) as part of NIJ's effort to promote the use of deoxyribonucleic acid (DNA) testing. Specifically, the study addressed two research questions:

- What are the current practices of law enforcement agencies with respect to investigating cold cases?
- What strategies can agencies use, based on the likelihood of success, to prioritize cold-case investigations?

A national survey of law enforcement agencies was used to determine whether and how agencies conducted cold-case investigations, while samples were drawn from investigative case files in four cities to determine attributes of cold cases that are associated with case clearance, arrest, and conviction.

The report is intended for an audience of researchers and criminal justice practitioners interested in policing and forensic issues. Other RAND work in this area includes *Toward a Comparison of DNA Profiling and Databases in the United States and England* (Goulka et al., 2010).

The RAND Center on Quality Policing

This research was conducted in the RAND Center on Quality Policing within the Safety and Justice Program of RAND Infrastructure, Safety, and Environment (ISE). The center conducts research and analysis to improve contemporary police practice and policy. The mission of ISE

[1] No universal definition of *cold case* currently exists; the criteria utilized by the joint FBI/District of Columbia Metropolitan Police Department Cold Case Homicide Squad in the early 1990s contains elements utilized by many agencies: "Cases are at least 1 year old and could not be addressed by the original homicide squad because of workload, time constraints, or the lack of viable leads" (Regini, 1997).

is to improve the development, operation, use, and protection of society's essential physical assets and natural resources and to enhance the related social assets of safety and security of individuals in transit and in their workplaces and communities. Safety and Justice Program research addresses all aspects of public safety and the criminal justice system—including violence, policing, corrections, substance abuse, and public integrity.

Questions or comments about this report should be sent to the lead author, Robert Davis (Robert_Davis@rand.org). Information about the Safety and Justice Program is available online (http://www.rand.org/ise/safety), as is information about the Center on Quality Policing (http://cqp.rand.org). Inquiries about research projects should be sent to the following address:

Greg Ridgeway, Director
Safety and Justice Program
RAND Corporation
1776 Main Street
P.O. Box 2138
Santa Monica, CA 90407-2138
310-393-0411, x7734
sjdirector@rand.org

Contents

Figures

Tables

Summary

Introduction

With modern clearance rates (which represent the proportion of cases solved divided by the number of cases opened during a given time period) far below those in the 1960s and DNA forensic technology having improved, law enforcement agencies have shown increasing interest in attempting to solve homicides and other serious crimes that seemed intractable during initial investigation, in what are called *cold-case investigations*. Fueled by the popularity of television shows focusing on forensic investigation, such cold-case investigations have captured the imagination of the American public, and cold-case investigations have become increasingly commonplace in law enforcement agencies.

Yet, despite the increasing number of cold-case units and the expenditure of significant resources to fund them, we know virtually nothing about the return on this investment. Does it make sense for law enforcement agencies to devote significant resources to solving cold cases, or are those resources better deployed in solving recent cases? How can agencies best organize and support cold-case work? What kinds of cold cases are most susceptible to being solved? What is the payoff to solving a cold case: Does solving a case always lead to arrest, prosecution, and conviction?

To better understand the efficacy of the cold-case investigations, we conducted a research study designed to address the following two objectives:

- Assess current practices in cold-case investigations and agency policies and procedures, and determine which are most effective in solving cold cases.
- Determine which types of cases are most likely to be solved, and develop models, based on case characteristics, for prioritizing cold-case investigations.

To address these two objectives, we relied on a two-step approach. We started by developing and fielding a national-level Internet survey of police and sheriffs' departments to determine organizational characteristics associated with cold-case solvability. The national survey was then used to help us identify four large metropolitan police agencies with cold-case units—the District of Columbia, Baltimore, and Dallas, where the focus was on cold-case homicides, and Denver, where the focus was on sexual-assault cases—that we visited. Working with the cold-case units in the four agencies, we examined cold-case files to try to identify which case and investigative variables are associated with clearance.

Key Findings from the National Cold-Case Survey

Of the 5,000 surveys mailed out, 1,051 were completed—for a response rate of about 20 percent. Based on the survey responses, the following emerge as key findings on current cold-case practice in law enforcement agencies:

- Most agencies do little cold-case work, with only 20 percent having a protocol for initiating cold-case investigations, 10 percent having dedicated cold-case investigators, and 7 percent having a formal cold-case unit.
- Cold-case funding is tenuous: Twenty percent of cold-case work is funded through line items in the budget, with most funded by grants or supplemental funds.
- Success rates for cold-case investigations are low: About one in five cases cleared; respondents estimated that one in 20 cold-case investigations resulted in arrest and that one in 100 cold-case investigations resulted in conviction.
- Agency factors associated with higher clearance rates included level of funding and access to investigative databases.

As noted, the survey findings are based on 1,051 returns from 5,000 surveys mailed out. Although this makes extrapolation from the sample data questionable, it is likely that many agencies that did not conduct any significant number of cold-case investigations saw little reason to complete a survey that centered completely on the process of conducting cold-case investigations. For this reason, the survey findings on the proportion of agencies that have dedicated cold-case investigators or units or formal protocols are best regarded as upper limits.

Key Findings from the Analysis of Cold-Case Files

Working with each of the four sites, we reviewed up to 200 case files of solved and unsolved cases that have been assigned to cold-case squads and extracted attributes of the crime and of the investigation that affected cold-case solvability. Based on that examination, the following key findings emerged:

- One can identify factors that predict whether a cold-case investigation will be successful, including the basis for initiating the cold-case investigation (e.g., family pressure, passage of time since crime occurred); characteristics of the victim and crime (e.g., age of case, location of body, victim age and gender, victim known to be a drug user); progress made during the initial investigation (e.g., known motivation for the crime, identification of a suspect during the initial investigation); and actions of cold-case investigators (e.g., developing a new theory of the crime and suspect motivation and conducting lineups).
- Clearing a cold case does not automatically lead to making an arrest. A substantial portion of successful investigations in all sites (from one in three to one in two) did not result in an arrest for a variety of reasons, including the inability to locate witnesses, uncooperative witnesses, a suspect being deceased or incarcerated, or DNA results that implicated multiple individuals or were otherwise inconclusive.
- In sexual-assault cold cases, even when a suspect DNA match has been made, about one-third of cases are not filed because of problems with victim cooperation, credibility, or

availability of suspects who are deceased or in prison. However, those cases that are prosecuted resulted in convictions and lengthy prison terms more than 90 percent of the time.
- Cooperation between police and prosecutors can improve both the efficiency and effectiveness of cold-case investigations. Typically, a prosecutor is not brought into the picture until a cold-case investigation has produced results. But, when police consult with prosecutors beginning at case screening, as they do in Denver, prosecutors can offer advice on whether the case is likely to produce a conviction if cleared and on what kinds of evidence will be most compelling in court.

We note that the three homicide sites that we selected for case-file work were chosen for reasons of convenience, access, and feasibility; they were not chosen randomly from among the 12 agencies that we identified from our Internet survey. We do not know whether findings from these sites are representative of agencies that conduct a high volume of cold-case investigations. Also, because we needed to rely on staff at the four sites for a selection of the cases, we cannot know whether the cases we received were representative of the entire set of cold-case investigations. However, because the numbers we requested represented a large proportion of cold cases worked at each site, the samples are likely fairly representative of cold-case investigations for each jurisdiction sampled.

Conclusions and Recommendations

According to this research, there are three types of cold-case investigations. The first type is the classic cold-case investigation, in which a detective picks up a case file because of a family or media inquiry or during a procedural review of cases that have remained unsolved for a specified length of time. These are the least common types of cold-case investigations.

The second type is based on availability of forensic tests. Forensic material from old cases once thought not to be amenable to DNA testing might now be testable due to advances in DNA technology. Federal funds are making this type of cold-case investigation increasingly common.

The third type consists of those cases opened because an individual charged with a crime confesses to the outstanding crime as part of a plea deal or because an eyewitness announces a willingness to finger a suspect in return for leniency after the witness is arrested for participating in a crime.

Each of these types of investigations has implications for cost and for the likelihood of success. The first type is likely to incur the highest costs and to have a low rate of success, even if judged by the lenient standard of exceptional clearances. Submitting or resubmitting DNA material for laboratory testing (the second type of case) is relatively inexpensive (the initial investment is the cost of DNA laboratory processing), but the rate of success from indiscriminant DNA testing of large numbers of cases is likely to be well below 50 percent. The third type of case involves little new investigation, and the cost of investigation is low. If the criterion for success is clearance, all such cases result in at least an exceptional clearance (one in which a suspect has been conclusively identified and evidence collected but prosecution is impossible because the offender is unavailable—is dead, is in prison, is unable to be located, or has entered into a plea bargain that precludes prosecution in the cold case), and a large majority are also likely to result in conviction. Assessments of the value of cold cases need to draw these distinctions when estimating the value of investments made in resources to investigate cold cases.

Also, some of our findings echo the findings of a mid-1970s RAND study of investigations from the 1970s (Chaiken, Greenwood, and Petersilia, 1976; Greenwood, Chaiken, and Petersilia, 1977). Like the authors of the earlier RAND work, we found that systems that monitor investigations and investigators' actions are either weak or nonexistent. Both studies also found that investigators were oriented toward clearing cases rather than winning convictions in court. These similarities after 35 years are striking.

We come away from our investigation having more questions than answers about cold-case investigations. We were surprised at the lack of accountability in cold-case work. Specifically, there is little emphasis on convictions as a goal of cold-case investigations. If obtaining a conviction were the ultimate goal, then it would seem logical for cold-case investigators to work closely with prosecutors when screening cases so they could decide whether, if the case were to be solved, there would likely be a prosecutable case. This is the model that was being used in the Denver site for the sexual-assault cold-case project. Police investigators sat down with prosecutors to determine whether each case that had material that could be submitted for DNA testing was likely to result in a conviction, assuming that a Combined DNA Index System (CODIS) hit would be made on suspect DNA.

Also, we did not see evidence that cold-case units were tracking conviction rates or other basic information on the efficacy and efficiency of cold-case investigations. Agencies had basic statistics on the number of cold cases worked, the number cleared by arrest, and the number of exceptional clearances. But they did not generally have information on court filings, convictions, sentences, or the time spent on cold-case investigations relative to the number of clearances obtained. For agencies in which there is a fixed number of dedicated cold-case investigators, it is relatively straightforward to divide the hours worked by number of cases cleared. However, we observed that the number of cold-case investigators is not always fixed and that detectives switch back and forth between active and cold-case investigations.

After reviewing these results, we suggest two topics that should be researched to better understand the potential for cold-case investigations.

Conduct a Cost-Effectiveness Analysis of Investigator Time Spent on Cold Cases Versus New Cases

Because of the paucity of data on cold-case investigations, we know little about the return on investment of investigative resources put into cold cases relative to active cases. For a police agency with a fixed investigation budget, the question of what proportion of resources should be diverted to cold cases is a practical decision with important consequences. Collecting information from several selected agencies would help inform those decisions. Using the data collected, it would be possible to develop cost-effectiveness models that relate the average amount of time spent on active and cold-case investigations to clearances and arrests. The models would specify the expected number of clearances and arrests per hour of effort expended on active case and cold-case investigations.

Assess the Conviction Rate for Cold Cases, and Determine Whether Prosecutor Involvement in Investigations Leads to a Higher Rate of Convictions

From a sample of agencies that conduct a large number of cold-case investigations, one could determine the conviction rate for successful cold-case investigations (i.e., those investigations that resulted in a clearance), what proportion of cleared cases are filed, and what proportion of the filings result in convictions. It would also be useful to collect reasons prosecutors gave for not filing cases and reasons for dismissal stated in prosecutor files for those cases that were filed but later dismissed. Interviews with detectives and prosecutors would provide further insight into the most-common reasons that cleared cold cases do not result in a conviction.

Acknowledgments

We would like to thank the members of our advisory committee, who provided helpful insights and assisted us in designing the research project:

- Charles Wellford, University of Maryland
- Art Westveer, Guardian Consultants
- Captain Michael Farris, District of Columbia Metropolitan Police Department
- Kaylyn Dueker, Naval Criminal Investigative Service
- Frederick A. Bornhofen, Vidocq Society
- James Gannon, Morris County, N.J., Prosecutor's Office
- Donald E. Steinhice, Baltimore City State's Attorney's Office.

Special thanks are due to Brett Chapman at NIJ for his support throughout the project.

Abbreviations

ADA	assistant district attorney
BJS	Bureau of Justice Statistics
CODIS	Combined DNA Index System
DNA	deoxyribonucleic acid
DOJ	U.S. Department of Justice
DPD	Dallas Police Department
FBI	Federal Bureau of Investigation
FTE	full-time equivalent
IACP	International Association of Chiefs of Police
IAFIS	Integrated Automated Fingerprint Identification System
LEO	Law Enforcement Online
MO	modus operandi
MPD	District of Columbia Metropolitan Police Department
NIJ	National Institute of Justice
RISS	Regional Information Sharing Systems
URL	uniform resource locator
VICAP	Violent Criminal Apprehension Program

CHAPTER ONE

Introduction

Background

Cold cases are among the most difficult that investigators confront. For a variety of reasons—lack of evidence, strained resources, ineffective investigation—a case becomes cold when initial efforts to solve it prove futile. Clearance rates for homicides and other serious crimes are far below what they were 50 years ago.[1] Lackluster rates of solution, combined with new technologies, such as deoxyribonucleic acid (DNA) and automated fingerprint matching, have prompted the police to form cold-case units, designed to address cases that stubbornly resist solution. In this chapter, we discuss this background in more detail.

Declining Clearance Rates

Until recently, the police enjoyed a high solvability rate for many types of crime. In those times of high clearance rates, it was thought that investigators contributed little to solving cases (Eck, 1979). Instead, cases "cleared themselves" through the efforts of patrol officers and citizen witnesses. A groundbreaking study by researchers from the RAND Corporation (Greenwood, Chaiken, and Petersilia, 1977; Chaiken, Greenwood, and Petersilia, 1976) found that 80 percent of cases were solved at the crime scene by actions of responding officers or by information about the identity of the perpetrator supplied by a victim or witness. Moreover, even those cases that were turned over to detective units received little investigation: Just 3 percent of index crimes (the eight major crimes that the FBI combines to produce its annual crime index) were solved by true investigative efforts.

However, the view of the role of investigations began to change as homicide clearance rates declined; they have decreased from 91 percent in 1965 to 63 percent today (Davies, 2007; Alderden and Lavery, 2007). By the mid-1990s, the problem of falling clearance rates had become acute. Criminologists and practitioners offered a variety of explanations for the lack of success in solving homicides. Many claimed that the nature of crime, especially violent crime, had changed. Gilbert (1983) attributed the 170-percent increase in homicides in San Diego from 1970 to 1980 to the rapid growth of stranger-on-stranger homicides. Cardarelli and Cavanagh (1992) found that 95 percent of unsolved homicides involved stranger or unknown relationships: In the early 1960s, the vast majority of homicide cases involved individuals who knew one another, but, by 1992, 53 percent of all murders were between strangers. A variety of studies support the assertion that stranger-on-stranger homicides are the most difficult to

[1] *Clearance* can be defined in a variety of ways; for example, with regard to homicide, one widely accepted definition holds that a case is cleared when one of the following occurs: an arrest is made, the suspect commits suicide contemporaneously with the homicide, or the homicide is ruled to be in self-defense (Wellford et al., 1999).

solve (see, for example, Rojek, 1996). Gilbert (1983) and Richardson and Kosa (2001) argue that the increase in the proportion of homicides that involve strangers has been especially acute in urban areas.

Other explanations for falling clearance rates also center on a change in the nature of homicides. The increased use of firearms in homicides—a means less likely to leave the suspect's tissue at the crime scene—has also been cited as having an affect on police detectives' ability to clear homicide cases (McDowall, 1991; Ousey and Lee, 2010). Along the same lines, Addington (2006) and Litwin (2004) found that weapon type affected clearance rates and that homicides in which firearms were used were less likely to be solved than were homicides involving no firearms. Riedel and Rinehart (1994, 1996) found that cases involving concomitant felonies—which were more common in the 1990s than in the 1960s—were substantially less likely to be solved than simple murders. The 1995 International Association of Chiefs of Police (IACP) Murder Summit (IACP, 1995) attributed the decline in murder clearances in part to increases in the percentage of murders that were related to gangs or drugs. Ousey and Lee (2010) found that the decline in homicides stemming from arguments was associated with the decline in clearance rates. Body location has also been identified as a factor affecting clearance rates (Litwin, 2004). Xu (2008) found that the increase in the percentage of homicides in which the body is found in a vehicle could have contributed to the decline in clearance rates.

Beyond changes in the nature of homicides, there are other reasons for the decline in clearance rates over time. Riedel and Jarvis (1999) concluded that witnesses' fear of retaliation or their distrust of the police was a major factor in the decline in clearance rates. People—especially in poor, high-crime neighborhoods—have become less trusting of law enforcement and, thus, unwilling to provide necessary information to solve homicides (Borg and Parker, 2001). Members of the country's growing immigrant population are often unwilling to come forward because they fear authorities or fear being deported. In contrast, in smaller, more–closely knit communities where most people know each other, authorities experience more success in obtaining information from the community about homicide (Weisheit and Wells, 2005; Paré, Felson, and Ouimet, 2007). Other researchers have also cited a lack of witnesses as an important explanatory variable for lower rates of clearance (Cordner, 1989; Riedel, 1995b, 1994; Forst et al., 1982).

How Agency Attributes Affect Clearance Rates

As caseloads rose and clearance rates fell in the 1980s and 1990s, policing experts began to think about how actions of patrol officers and investigators might make a difference in solving crimes (Eck, 1983; Forst et al., 1982; Willman and Snortum, 1984; Regini, 1997; Thompson, 2000; Thompson, Chinoy, and Vobejda, 2000; Vobejda and Chinoy, 2000; Ahlberg and Knutsson, 1987; Greenwood, Chaiken, and Petersilia, 1977; McEwen, 2009; Hsu, 2007). One line of research investigated how attributes of police agencies and investigative units were related to clearance rates.

In a major study of homicide clearance rates, Wellford et al. (1999) found sizable and relatively stable differences in clearance rates between individual jurisdictions. They concluded that "there are variables affecting clearance rates . . . that are constant. Identifying these variables related to high levels of clearance could help improve police practices and the ability of departments to clear serious crimes" (pp. 2–3).

As far back as the mid-1970s, Bloch and Bell (1976) noted that investigative decentralization and case screening led to higher arrest and clearance rates for the targeted crimes of burglary, robbery, and larceny. Although Elliott (1978) found a positive relationship between team policing and clearance rates, Gay, Day, and Woodward (1977) met with mixed results in their study of team policing in 18 U.S. cities. Schwartz and Clarren (1977) likewise determined that team policing yielded positive results in terms of burglary reduction. Cordner (1989) found that clearance rates decrease as agency size increases, presumably because characteristics of rural areas and their agencies made it easier to solve a larger proportion of crimes. According to Cordner, the region in the state and the mix of crimes reported to the police appeared to have the greatest effect on clearance: The greater the proportion of property crimes, the lower the rate of clearance. Keel, Jarvis, and Muirhead (2009) found that the use of such sophisticated analytical tools as blood splatter, criminal investigative analysis, and voice stress analysis in interviews increased clearance rates.

In an extensive review of literature, Rinehart (1994) considered such factors as personnel assignment, caseload, investigator skill, training, officer age, experience, gender, deployment, case closure features, resources, community relations, management, deployment and use of other policing units, thoroughness of investigation, information processing technologies, and department organization. She concluded that few organizational variables significantly affect clearance rates; rather, police–community relations and characteristics of the community have the greatest effect.

Today, there is a growing body of literature on how to improve investigative techniques to maximize the number of cases solved. Some studies have found a positive relationship between case clearance and organizational variables, such as detective experience and expenditures (Borg and Parker, 2001; National Institute of Justice [NIJ], 1997), but this finding is not consistently supported in all studies (see, e.g., Puckett and Lundman, 2003; Greenwood and Petersilia, 1975). Procedures followed at the initial response and crime scene were found to be important in multiple studies. More specifically, cases are more likely to be solved when the first responding officers contact the homicide unit, medical examiner's office, and the crime lab; when they immediately secure the crime scene; when they search for witnesses; and when the detectives arrive within 30 minutes of crime-scene discovery (Wellford et al., 1999). Similarly, successful outcomes are more likely when multiple detectives are assigned to a case (at least three or more); when computer database checks are run on all parties and evidence (victim, suspect, witnesses, and weapons); and when thorough interviews are conducted with witnesses, family members, acquaintances, and neighbors of the witnesses (Riedel and Rinehart, 1996; Schroeder and White, 2009; Baskin and Sommers, 2010).

The Ascendancy of DNA

At the same time that clearance rates fell, the introduction of DNA testing in the 1980s brought about a major revolution in criminal investigations. Historically, matching an individual to a crime required eyewitness identification or the matching of specific body characteristics, such as fingerprints or dental records. The introduction of DNA evidence has allowed offenders to be identified by analyzing unique nucleic information found in any part of the human body (Gans and Urbas, 2002). DNA samples can be as small as a drop of blood or saliva, a strand of hair, or skin cells from a handled object (Federal Judicial Center, 2000).

DNA provides a high degree of certainty that evidence left at a crime scene does or does not belong to a particular individual. Its early use was either to exonerate or to strengthen the case against an individual who had already been identified as a suspect in a crime (Golding et al., 2000).

However, crime experts quickly realized that DNA could be used to identify suspects in cases in which no suspect had been identified through other investigative means. The federal government began developing a system of national, state, and local DNA databases in the late 1980s, called the Combined DNA Index System (CODIS). CODIS links 50 state databases and local databases from around the country and allows localities to submit DNA samples to match against the database. The convicted-offender index contains DNA profiles of individuals convicted of particular crimes, while the forensic index contains DNA profiles collected from evidence at crime scenes. When a profile is submitted, CODIS uses software to search across the different tiers and indexes to locate a match (NIJ, 2003).

Today, all 50 states and the federal government have statutes requiring that DNA samples be taken from certain classes of offenders (U.S. House of Representatives, 2003). Individual states have also gradually expanded the population of criminals from whom DNA samples are taken. All 50 states require DNA samples from convicted murderers and sex offenders, and 46 states require samples from persons convicted of any violent offense (Lovrich et al., 2004). In the past few years, states have increasingly begun to require samples from nonviolent-felony offenders as well. Today, 45 states require DNA samples from convicted burglars, 36 from convicted drug offenders, and 31 from all convicted felons (Lovrich et al., 2004). In addition, four states now require that DNA samples be taken at the time of arrest. However, because of civil liberty concerns, samples from arrestees currently are not used in the national database.

Proponents point to successful use of DNA evidence to solve serial crimes, including the infamous Green River killings in Washington (U.S. House of Representatives, 2003). Case studies have highlighted numerous serious crimes that could have been avoided if DNA testing had been available (Lovrich et al., 2004). A recent NIJ study suggested that even submitting casework DNA samples from property-crime scenes can result in links to other crimes and leads to violent offenders (NIJ, 2004).

The Growth of Cold-Case Squads

By the late 1980s, the sheer volume of unsolved cases had become overwhelming for many agencies. In addition, the promise of technologies, such as DNA and automated fingerprint matching, convinced police administrators that old unsolved cases that sat neglected might benefit from a fresh perspective. Although the concept of cold-case investigations predated the 1980s, that decade saw an increase in the creation of cold-case squads in response to the rising number of cold cases and the availability of new means to tackle them (Regini, 1997).

Although originally begun to address unsolved homicides, cold-case squads quickly expanded to include sexual assault; today, some jurisdictions even use the cold-case squads to investigate property crimes. In addition to using new technologies, other cold-case strategies include focusing intensive resources at a single case, using new personnel to provide a "fresh" perspective, and leveraging the use of outside resources (e.g., conducting criminal investigative analysis [behavioral profiling] or submitting the case to the Federal Bureau of Investigation's [FBI's] Violent Criminal Apprehension Program [VICAP]).

There is wide variability in how cold-case investigations are carried out. For example, there is no universally accepted metric for when a case becomes "cold." Many jurisdictions arbitrarily use the passage of a year as a boundary, but recent research suggests that there is a sharp decline in the ability to solve after 72 hours has passed (Regoeczi, Jarvis, and Riedel, 2008). This suggests that unsolved cases might benefit from cold-case techniques employed at an earlier stage of the investigation.

There is also wide variability in how cold-case squads are administered, staffed, organized, and resourced. Some smaller jurisdictions do not field standing units; instead, single investigators pursue cold cases on an ad hoc basis as a collateral duty. In other areas, there are multijurisdictional task forces with federal, state, and local representation, organized much like the FBI's Joint Terrorism Task Forces. And, although there are many anecdotal reports of success, often sensationally showcased in the popular media (see NIJ, 2002), it is not clear at present that cold-case squads are either effective or efficient.

Despite the growing number of cold-case investigative units and the expenditure of significant resources to fund them, we know virtually nothing about the return on this investment. Does it make sense for law enforcement agencies to devote significant resources to solving cold cases, or are those resources better deployed in solving recent cases? How can agencies best organize and support cold-case work? What kinds of cold cases are most susceptible to being solved? What is the payoff to solving a cold case: Does solving a case always lead to an arrest, prosecution, and conviction?

Objectives and Approach

This study was designed to help begin answering these questions by adding to our knowledge of how cold-case work is organized and funded and of what factors are likely to produce a successful investigation. The goal of this analysis is to provide guidance to local, state, and federal officials about resource allocation, agency organization, and case selection in optimizing case clearance.

This report has two objectives. The first one is to assess current practices in cold-case investigations and agency policies and procedures and determine which are most effective in solving cold cases. We know very little about how much cold-case investigations are being conducted by law enforcement agencies or how this work is being carried out. Key questions we address include the following: Do a large number of agencies have dedicated cold-case investigators or policies on when cold-case investigations are to be opened and how the investigations are to be conducted? Do differences in organization of cold-case work and levels of funding of cold-case investigations produce differences in clearance rates?

The second objective is to determine which types of cases are most likely to be solved, and develop models for prioritizing cold-case investigations based on case characteristics. As suggested in the background section of this chapter, there has been empirical work on how case attributes and investigator actions affect clearance rates for homicide and other crimes. However, we do not know whether findings from these studies can be applied to cold-case investigations. Cold cases are emphatically *not* a representative sample of all crimes, so it is not clear whether the same rules apply to cold cases as apply to other cases. If we could identify case attributes and investigative actions associated with a higher likelihood of clearance, then guidelines could be established to give agencies an idea of which cases are most likely to be solved if an investment of resources is expended on a cold-case investigation.

To address these objectives, we used different approaches for each objective. To address the first objective, we developed and fielded a national online survey of law enforcement agencies to document the range of ways in which cold-case work is conducted and assess how this organization affects cold-case clearance rates.

The national survey was used as the basis for the second approach, which was used to address the second objective. Specifically, it was used to identify four jurisdictions that conduct large numbers of cold-case investigations. We chose three jurisdictions that conducted a large number of cold-case homicide investigations—the District of Columbia, Baltimore, and Dallas. To these three sites, we added Denver because it received a U.S. Department of Justice (DOJ) grant to conduct testing of DNA material in sexual-assault cold cases. For each site, we reviewed up to 200 case files of solved and unsolved cases that have been assigned to cold-case squads and extracted attributes of the crime and of the investigation that affected cold-case solvability.

More detail on the approaches used for each objective is included later in this report.

Study Limitations

In conducting the study, there were some potential problems with both the survey and case-file study samples that could limit our findings. As we discuss in more detail in Chapter Two, the survey response rate was low. We do not know whether this reflects apathy or confusion on the part of the agencies that received the survey or whether agencies that placed little or no emphasis on cold-case investigations simply did not see a reason to return a survey that dealt with how cold-case investigations were conducted. Regardless of the reason, the low response rate does limit the generalizability of the findings. We provide more discussion of our approach and the limitations in Chapter Two.

In terms of the case-study sites, the three homicide sites that we selected for case-file work were chosen for reasons of convenience, access, and feasibility; they were not chosen randomly from among the 12 agencies that we identified from our Internet survey. We do not know whether findings from these sites are representative of agencies that conduct a high volume of cold-case investigations. We provide more discussion of our approach and the limitations in Chapter Three.

Organization of This Report

The remainder of this report is organized around the analyses to address the two study objectives. In Chapter Two, we discuss the Internet survey we fielded and conducted to address the first objective and then present the results of that analysis. Appendix A contains a copy of the survey instrument used. In Chapter Three, we discuss the case-study site approach we used to address the second objective, followed by a discussion of the results. Appendix B contains a copy of the cold-case data-abstraction form we used in our site visits to the agencies. In Chapter Four, we provide conclusions and offer some recommendations.

CHAPTER TWO

Assessing Current Practices in Cold-Case Investigations

Because we know very little about how many cold-case investigations are being conducted by law enforcement agencies or how this work is being carried out, our first study objective sought to assess current practices in cold-case investigations and agency policies and procedures and determine which are most effective in solving cold cases. To accomplish that objective, we developed and fielded a law enforcement survey over the Internet.

In this chapter, we discuss our approach in developing and fielding the survey and the results from analyzing the survey.

Approach to Assessing Current Practices in Cold-Case Investigations

To get at our first study objective, we developed a law enforcement survey; a copy of the final survey instrument is included as Appendix A. The survey was developed with the assistance of an expert scientific review panel that included several cold-case investigators. More specifically, the expert panel consisted of the following individuals:

- Charles Wellford, University of Maryland
- Art Westveer, Guardian Consultants
- Captain Michael Farris, District of Columbia Metropolitan Police Department (MPD)
- Kaylyn Dueker, Naval Criminal Investigative Service
- Fred Bornhofen, Vidocq Society
- Jimmy Gannon, Morris County, N.J., Prosecutor's Office
- Don Steinhice, Baltimore City State's Attorney's Office.

A draft of the survey instrument was produced in advance of the advisory panel meeting, and members of the advisory panel discussed the draft and made suggestions. The penultimate version of the survey was submitted to NIJ for comments prior to finalizing it.

The developed web-based survey was fielded by the University of Baltimore's Schaefer Center for Public Policy. In determining whom to send the survey to, the center started from a Bureau of Justice Statistics (BJS) database of chiefs of police and sheriffs. This original database was comprised of 15,884 chiefs of police from all police departments in the United States, including Native American tribal police departments.

The center then drew a stratified sample of 5,000 agencies from the original database, as shown in Table 2.1. The resulting sample of 5,000 included Native American tribal police departments (44) and all other departments with more than 100 full-time sworn officers (997).

Table 2.1
Sample Composition by Agency Size

Agency Category	Sample Size
Tribal	44
1–25 sworn full-time officers	1,886
26–50 sworn full-time officers	1,000
51–75 sworn full-time officers	707
76–99 sworn full-time officers	366
100 or more sworn full-time officers	997

The balance of the sample (3,959) was comprised of police departments in the following size categories: 1,886 from departments with zero to 25 full-time sworn officers; 1,000 from departments with 26 to 50 full-time sworn officers; 707 from departments with 51 to 75 full-time sworn officers; and 366 from departments with 76 to 99 full-time sworn officers. The center administered the web-based survey using Sawtooth Technologies' Sensus web survey software.

On November 17, 2008, the chiefs of police in the sample were sent a letter explaining the purpose of the survey and inviting them to participate. Potential respondents were directed to the web-based survey instrument through a provided web address (uniform resource locator, or URL). Three separate mailings were made. The first mailing went to all 5,000 respondents. Two weeks later, letters were mailed to the 4,919 respondents who had not yet completed the survey. Two weeks after the second letter was sent, letters were mailed to the 4,570 respondents who had not yet completed the survey. The survey was taken down from the web in February 2009.

Of the 5,000 surveys mailed out, 1,051 were completed—for a response rate of about 20 percent. Nine hundred fifty-nine of the returns were fully completed, and the remaining 92 were partially completed. We broke down responses according to type of agency, size of agency, and region of the United States. Response rates varied little by agency type. Nineteen percent of police agencies returned surveys, a percentage that is virtually identical to the percentages of other types of agencies that returned surveys: 18 percent of sheriff offices, 20 percent of state police agencies, and 14 percent of tribal police agencies.

Neither did we find substantial differences according to region of the country. We received returns from 17 percent of respondents in the Northeast, 25 percent of agencies in the Southeast, 21 percent of agencies in the North Central region, 16 percent of agencies in the South Central region, and 21 percent of agencies in the Northwest. Only the southwestern states, which returned 32 percent of surveys mailed out, had a response rate that stood out from the others.

We did note that there was a moderate correlation between agency size and response rate. Surveys were returned by 33 percent of agencies with 100 or more sworn officers, by 26 percent of agencies with 76 to 99 sworn officers, by 27 percent of agencies with 51 to 75 sworn officers, and by 20 percent of agencies with 26 to 50 sworn officers, but only by 12 percent of agencies with 25 or fewer sworn officers.

It is hard to know how confident we can be in extrapolating from the survey sample, given that most agencies that received surveys (around 80 percent) did not return them. Because the survey is focused completely on cold cases, one explanation for the low response rate is that agencies that do not routinely investigate cold cases are unlikely to have seen a reason to complete the survey. This explanation is bolstered by the substantially higher return rate among agencies with more than 100 sworn officers—those agencies most likely to conduct regular cold-case investigations. Although it is unlikely that the composition of the sample affects the dynamics of cold-case investigations (cold cases from responders are unlikely to look substantially different from cold cases of nonresponders), the low response rate and differences by agency size are likely to affect estimates of cold-case practices (e.g., the proportion of agencies that have a dedicated cold-case unit). For this reason, the estimates of the proportion of agencies having dedicated cold-case investigators, dedicated cold-case units, or defined cold-case protocols are best thought of as upper limits on the proportions of these characteristics in the law enforcement population.

Survey Results

In this section, we discuss our analysis of the survey results, starting with agency cold-case practices, how cold-case investigations are administered, and the cold-case investigations themselves.

Cold-Case Practices

The first questions asked survey respondents about how cases were closed. As shown in Figure 2.1, in most cases, the decision to close a case was made by the investigative supervisors (41 percent), by the case investigator (18 percent), or by a committee of investigators (3 percent). Thirty-six percent of respondents indicated that their agencies did not close cases—that is, cases remained open, but without active pursuit.

Seventy percent of respondents said that their agency had an articulated policy on reactivating and investigating cold cases. Those who responded affirmatively were asked whether

Figure 2.1
How Cases Are Closed, Percentage of All Cases

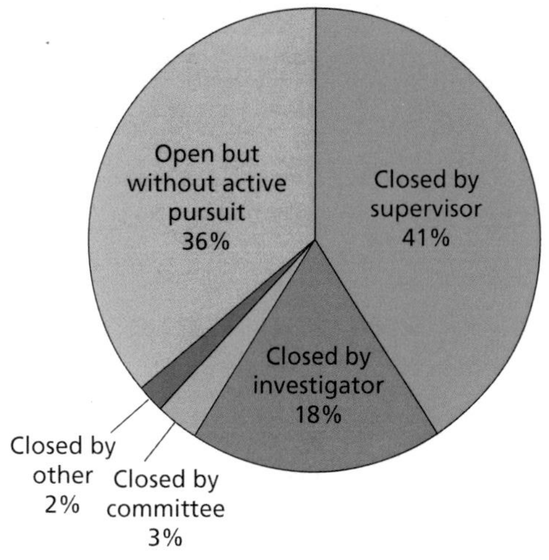

RAND *TR948-2.1*

their agency had a formal protocol for determining which cold cases to work, and 23 percent indicated that they did. We asked the 23 percent answering affirmatively to indicate the components of their protocol from a list composed by the cold-case investigators advising the study. Figure 2.2 indicates that the most-common elements of cold-case selection protocols were new witnesses coming forward (mentioned by 90 percent of respondents), availability of new DNA technology to test old physical evidence (also mentioned by 90 percent), availability of new material for DNA testing (mentioned by 86 percent), availability of other physical evidence (mentioned by 86 percent, and availability of new technology for non-DNA physical evidence (mentioned by 86 percent). Least mentioned aspects of protocols included overturning of a prior conviction (mentioned by 22 percent of respondents) and recovered memory or new information from previously known witnesses (mentioned by 36 percent). These responses strongly indicate that physical evidence is the major factor in decisions to reopen cold cases.

By far, the most–commonly worked cases were homicides: Sixty-eight percent of agencies had worked at least one cold homicide case during the past year, as shown in Table 2.2. The next most–commonly investigated cold cases were missing persons, with at least 35 percent of agencies investigating at least one missing-person case. Surprisingly, burglaries were the third most common type of cold-case investigation, followed by sex offenses (investigated by 29 percent of agencies) and robberies (investigated by 23 percent of agencies). The least commonly investigated cold-case crimes were embezzlement (investigated by 16 percent of agencies), arson (investigated by 15 percent of agencies), and kidnapping (investigated by 8 percent of agencies).

We calculated clearance rates for each category of cold cases worked (the right-most column of Table 2.2) by dividing the number of each type of case that respondents reported by the number they reported solved, and averaging the proportions across respondents. The cases fell into two groups: Sex offenses, burglaries, homicides, robberies, and missing persons were solved at a rate of roughly one in five, while embezzlement, arson, and kidnapping were

Figure 2.2
Factors Contributing to the Reopening of Cases

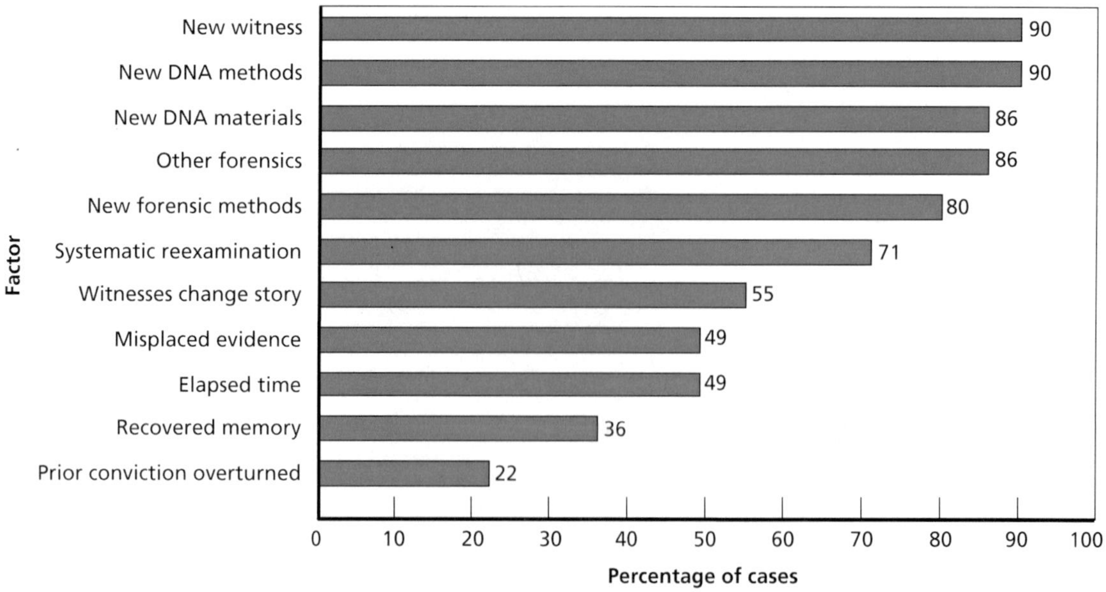

RAND *TR948-2.2*

Table 2.2
Types and Clearance Rates of Cold Cases Worked in the Past Year

Type of Crime	Percentage of Agencies That Worked at Least One Case in the Past Year	Clearance Rate (%)
Homicides	68	21
Missing persons	35	16
Burglaries	29	23
Sex offenses	29	24
Robberies	23	19
Embezzlement	16	7
Arson	15	5
Kidnapping	8	6

solved at rates of less than one in ten. The difference in clearance rates between the two groups of cases might be the result of the availability of DNA evidence for some cases in the former group. DNA material is not normally available to be tested in embezzlement, arson, or kidnapping cases.

Administration of Cold-Case Investigations

The next questions asked about administrative issues. According to respondents, 7 percent of agencies have formal cold-case units. (As mentioned earlier, based on the earlier discussion of likely survey responders, this figure represents an upper bound.) Not surprisingly, dedicated units are found almost exclusively in larger agencies (as shown in Figure 2.3). Less than 1 percent of agencies with 50 or fewer sworn officers had dedicated units. Yet, even among agencies with 100 or more sworn officers, at best, 18 percent have dedicated cold-case units.

Ten percent of respondents said that their agencies have dedicated cold-case investigators. More commonly, cold cases are assigned to the original lead investigator (20 percent of agen-

Figure 2.3
Formal Cold-Case Units, by Agency Size

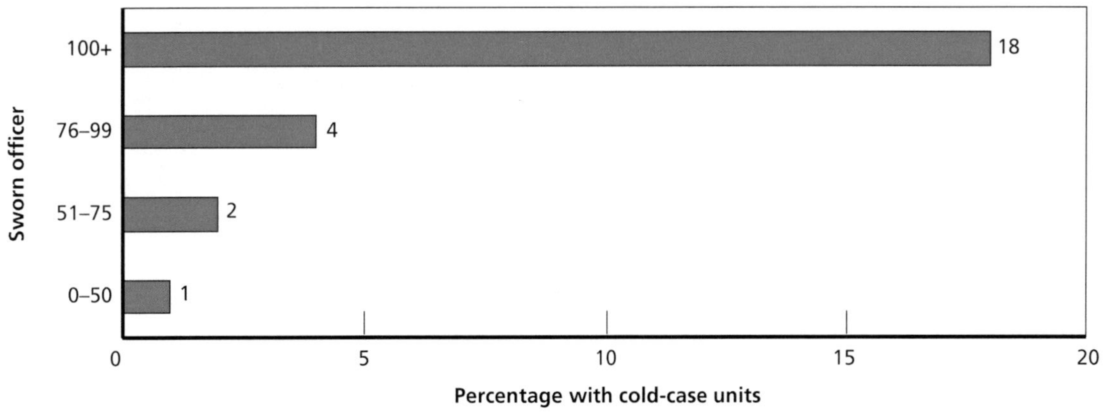

RAND *TR948-2.3*

cies) or assigned as part of detectives' regular workload (29 percent of agencies). A majority of agencies (54 percent) had two or fewer sworn full-time equivalents (FTEs) assigned to cold-case work, but one in ten had ten or more officers assigned. Nineteen percent also had at least one civilian FTE working on cold cases.

Most cold-case investigators had relatively small caseloads (as shown in Figure 2.4). Thirty-five percent reported caseloads of five cases or fewer, and more than half (54 percent) carried ten or fewer cases. At the other extreme, 4 percent claimed caseloads larger than 50. It seems likely that the large discrepancy in caseloads is the result of policies on case closure: Agencies that do not have policies limiting the length of cold-case investigations would be inclined to have investigators carrying large—but mostly inactive—caseloads.

According to survey respondents, 20 percent of cold-case work was funded through established line items in their agency's budget. A majority of cold-case investigations (56 percent) were funded by grants or supplemental agency funds. Of those agencies with a specific allocation of funds for cold cases, the median estimated by respondents was $35,000. Moreover, only half of the respondents from grant-funded units indicated that their agencies had committed to continued funding. From this, we conclude that cold-case units are relatively precarious. Because they are a fairly new concept, it is hard to say whether the uncertainty in their funding will change as time goes on.

Cold-Case Investigations

DNA Testing. We asked respondents about their agencies' practices in terms of DNA testing in cold cases. Agencies that had submitted DNA samples for testing reported an average (median) of about four cases during the past year. We next asked about "hits" from samples submitted. According to survey respondents, an average of 11 percent were matched and

Figure 2.4
Caseloads of Cold-Case Investigators

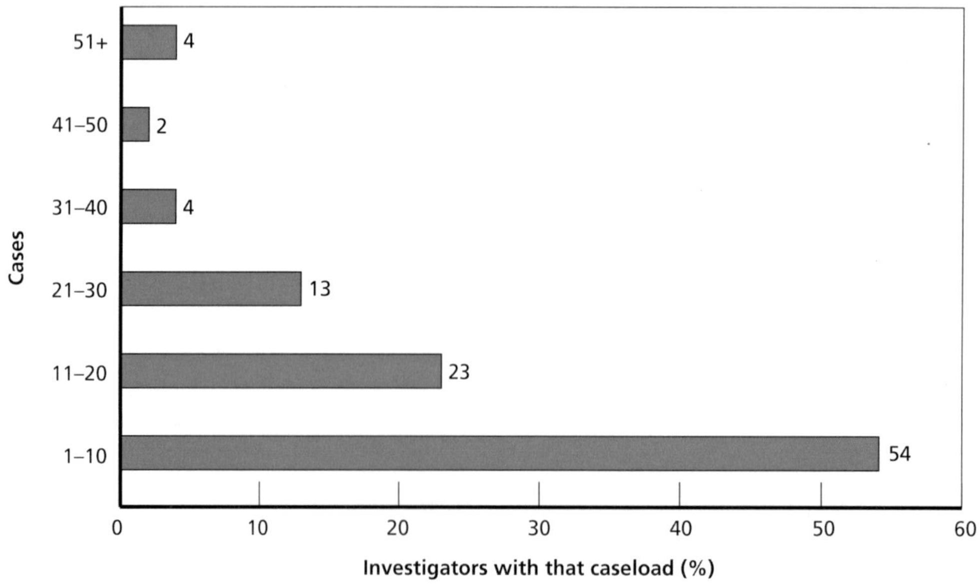

RAND *TR948-2.4*

resulted in identification of suspects. An average of 5 percent of samples tested were matched, linking the case to DNA material from other investigations.

Only 13 percent of agencies reported having specific policies on the types of cold cases or circumstances under which DNA samples are submitted for matching. Those that did have policies fell into several categories. One common policy was that DNA is submitted in certain types of cases—typically, part I crimes, violent crimes, homicides, or sexual assaults.[1] It was less common to submit DNA in all types of cases. Other agencies submitted samples based on circumstances, either in cases in which they felt that DNA evidence would be probative or in cases in which a suspect had been identified. A final group of agencies reported that whether to submit DNA evidence was a decision made by the local prosecutor.

Institutional Support. Some agencies lent various forms of institutional support to facilitate successful investigations (as shown in Figure 2.5). The most common type of institutional support was overtime pay with supervisory permission, noted by 37 percent of respondents. Other forms of common institutional support were funds to travel outside the jurisdiction to pursue leads (noted by 32 percent of respondents) and being able to take home a car (noted by 24 percent of respondents). Then again, only a small number of agencies reported that cold-case investigators were able to work overtime hours without authorization or that investigators received incentives for their work.

Respondents were then asked about strategies their agencies used to promote cold-case investigations (as shown in Figure 2.6). Among these, the most frequent one was assigning senior investigators to cold cases (mentioned by 45 percent of respondents). Participation in information sharing systems, such as Regional Information Sharing Systems (RISS) and Law Enforcement Online (LEO), was mentioned by 30 percent of respondents. Other strategies were less frequently employed, mentioned by fewer than one in five respondents. These

Figure 2.5
Types of Institutional Support for Cold-Case Investigators

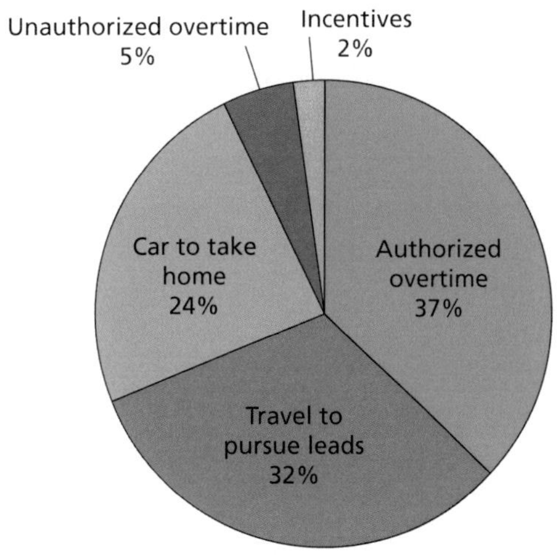

RAND *TR948-2.5*

---

[1] *Part I crimes* are defined as the eight most serious crimes: homicide, rape, aggravated assault, burglary, robbery, auto theft, theft, and arson.

Figure 2.6
Strategies to Promote Cold-Case Investigations

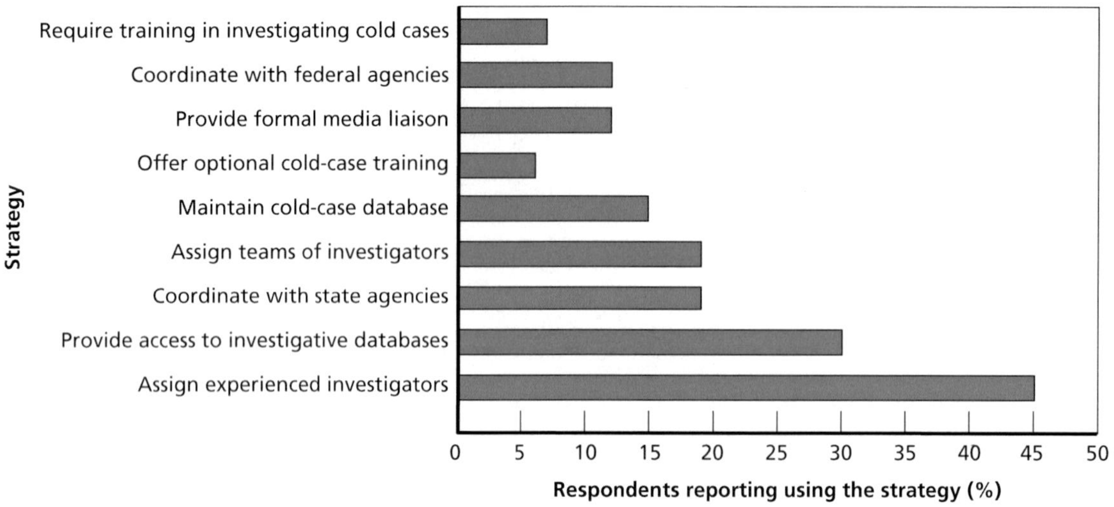

RAND *TR948-2.6*

included coordination with state law enforcement agencies, assigning teams of investigators, maintaining a cold-case database, offering elective specialized cold-case training, maintaining a formal liaison with the media, coordinating with federal agencies, and requiring specialized training in cold cases.

Agencies varied widely in the proportion of cold cases with a known perpetrator that resulted in arrest. Twenty-eight percent of respondents did not know what their cold-case arrest rate was, and fully one in three agencies that completed the survey (36 percent) reported making no cold-case arrests. These obviously tended to be agencies that conducted few cold-case investigations. Nearly two in three agencies (62 percent) reported arrests in 10 percent or less of cold cases investigated. However, 14 percent of agencies reported arrests in better than three-quarters of the cold cases in which a perpetrator had been identified. The median proportion of cases with a known perpetrator in which an arrest was made was a surprisingly low 5 percent. The median proportion of cases with a known perpetrator resulting in conviction, according to respondents, was less than 1 percent.

We conducted a multivariate analysis to determine whether we could identify factors associated with higher rates of cold-case arrests. We examined whether the arrest rate for cold cases was associated with each of the following factors:

- existence of a dedicated cold-case unit
- caseload of cold-case investigators
- level of finding for cold-case investigations
- receipt of DOJ grant for cold-case work
- types of institutional support (take-home cars, overtime pay, travel funding, incentives)
- agency cold-case strategies (see Figure 2.6).

We found statistically significant bivariate relationships between cold-case arrest rates and four of these factors: funding for cold-case investigations, access to investigative databases, travel funding, and existence of a media liaison for cold-case investigations. However, the relationships we found were weak, each explaining at most 10 percent of the variation in arrest rates. To determine the independent effects of each of these factors, we entered the factors into a regression model with arrest rate as the dependent variable. The only factor that exerted a statistically significant independent effect was the level of cold-case funding, which explained 6 percent of the variation in arrest rates.

Factors Affecting Cold-Case Investigation Decisions and Clearances. The final question in the survey was about factors that affect decisions about which cases merit cold-case investigations and which affect the likelihood that cold cases will be solved.[2] Respondents were asked to rate 19 factors on a scale of 1 (not important) to 5 (very important). The factors that respondents rated most highly for determining which cases are selected for active cold-case work were new information from witnesses or informants, availability of untested DNA material or fingerprints, availability of outstanding leads to pursue, and identification of a suspect (as shown in the middle column of Table 2.3). Least important were media attention paid to a case, whether the statute of limitations was about to expire, whether the original investigators and their notes were available, and queries from family members or the victim. Factors rated highly by respondents for solving cold cases (the right-most column) included availability of DNA material or fingerprints to be tested, new information from witnesses or informants, identification of a suspect, and availability of outstanding leads to pursue.

That factors affecting the decision to investigate and factors affecting cold-case clearance are congruent suggests that practical considerations, rather than social pressure, rule the decision about which cases to reopen and work as cold cases. This runs counter to things we have heard from experienced investigators, some of whom told us that inquiries from families and from the media are likely to draw renewed attention to cases. It might be that such inquiries do cause investigators to reexamine cases, but not necessarily to formally reopen them as full-fledged cold-case investigations, unless there are also good evidentiary leads to pursue.

Summary of Survey Results

The survey results showed that a relatively small proportion of responding agencies (7 percent) had dedicated cold-case units or had a formal protocol for determining which cold cases to investigate (14 percent). Those that do have dedicated units or formal protocols rely primarily on new witness information and newly testable physical evidence in deciding whether to reopen cases. Again, given the low response rate to the survey, the sample statistics represent upper bounds on these characteristics in the general population of law enforcement agencies.

By far, the most common type of cold case investigated is homicide, followed by sexual assault and burglary. Reported clearance rates for all types of cold-case investigations are about one in five.

Funding for cold cases appears tenuous. Most agencies do not include cold-case investigations as a line item in their budgets, and the median allocation of funds for cold-case investigations was $35,000.

Thirteen percent of agencies had policies about the types of cold cases in which DNA samples were submitted to crime labs for matching, most often submitting DNA samples in

---

[2] This question, which asks about *practices*, is somewhat different from the one presented in Figure 2.2 about agencies' *formal policies* for determining which cold cases to investigate.

Table 2.3
Factors That Affect Investigation and Clearance of Cold Cases

	Importance for Decision to Investigate		Importance for Solving	
Factor	**Rating**	**Rank**	**Rating**	**Rank**
New witness information provided	4.81	1	4.63	3
Availability of DNA evidence that could be submitted for CODIS or other database match	4.74	2	4.74	1
Other new information provided by citizens or informants	4.68	3	4.57	5
Availability of fingerprint evidence of IAFIS quality	4.67	4	4.68	2
Availability of outstanding leads to pursue	4.61	5	4.56	6
Murder weapon recovered	4.59	6	4.46	8
Suspect has been identified	4.51	7	4.61	4
Projectiles or casings recovered of quality to submit for database match	4.50	8	4.40	9
Potential of obtaining additional information from witnesses	4.43	9	4.47	7
Case fits pattern of serial crimes	4.37	10	4.18	13
Victim has been identified	4.13	11	4.32	11
Evidence has been properly handled and stored over course of investigation	4.11	12	4.37	10
Case file is complete and retrievable	4.01	13	4.26	12
Aggravating circumstances (innocence of victim, hate crime, heinousness of crime)	3.91	14	3.67	16
Original investigator case notes are available	3.62	15	3.87	14
Queries from family members or victim	3.61	16	3.23	17
Original investigators or responding officers are available for interview	3.39	17	3.73	15
Statute of limitations about to expire	3.24	18	3.15	18
Media attention paid to case	2.82	19	2.77	19

NOTE: IAFIS = Integrated Automated Fingerprint Identification System.

investigations involving violent crimes. On average, respondents reported that 10 percent of the DNA samples were matched to a suspect and that 5 percent were matched to another incident.

The most-common forms of institutional support lent by agencies to support cold-case work were overtime pay and travel to pursue leads. The most-frequent strategies employed by agencies to promote cold-case investigations were assigning senior investigators to work cold cases and providing access to investigative databases.

The median proportion of cases with a known perpetrator in which an arrest was made was reported to be small (5 percent), and the median proportion of convictions even smaller (1 percent). Examining a range of factors indicated that only the amount of funding provided for cold-case investigations affected the proportion of investigations that resulted in arrest and that that explained only 6 percent of the variation in arrest rates.

Finally, respondents indicated that cold cases were more likely to be opened when new information was available from witnesses or informants, when DNA evidence or fingerprints were newly available for testing, when there were outstanding leads to pursue, whether notes from the original investigation were available, or when a suspect had been identified. The same set of factors was judged by respondents to be those most likely to lead to clearing cold cases.

CHAPTER THREE

Case-File Analysis

As noted in Chapter One, there has been empirical work on how case attributes and investigator actions affect clearance rates for homicide and other crimes. However, we do not know whether findings from these studies can be applied to cold-case investigations. Thus, the second study objective was to determine which types of cases are most likely to be solved, then to develop models for prioritizing cold-case investigations based on case characteristics.

To accomplish this objective, we used the national survey discussed in Chapter Two to identify four jurisdictions that conduct large numbers of cold-case investigations. We chose three jurisdictions that conducted a large number of cold-case homicide investigations: the District of Columbia, Baltimore, and Dallas. To these three sites, we added Denver because it received a DOJ grant to conduct testing of DNA material in sexual-assault cold cases.

In this chapter, we first discuss the approach to doing the case-file analysis at the four sites and then discuss the results of that analysis. Appendix B contains a copy of the cold-case data-abstraction form we used in our site visits to the agencies.

Approach to Conducting Case-File Analysis

In this section, we discuss how we selected the sites, then briefly review each of the four sites selected.

Site Selection

As noted, we used the survey results to select sites for an analysis of case files. To ensure that we could obtain a large number of cases for our analysis, we looked at sites that reported conducting in excess of 50 cold-case investigations per year. There were a dozen agencies that reported conducting more than 50 investigations per year; from these, we selected the District of Columbia, Baltimore, and Dallas for our analyses. The selection of these sites was not made randomly; instead, it was based on considerations of travel distance, relationships with departments, and feasibility. (Two sites we had approached ultimately declined because the cost of locating and transporting files in storage was prohibitive.)

Because these three sites conducted many cold-case homicide investigations, we hoped to gain a better understanding of factors associated with cold-case solvability factors. We aimed to sample equal numbers of successful and unsuccessful cold-case investigations and abstract information from files to determine what factors distinguish the two types of cases.

To these three sites, we added Denver because it received a DOJ grant to conduct testing of DNA material in sexual-assault cold cases. The Denver sample consisted of cases in which a DNA match had been made. Thus, the research question in Denver was different from the question in the other three sites. Specifically, we wanted to know what the probability of an arrest, prosecution, and conviction was among cases in which there was a CODIS hit—in other words, in cases in which the perpetrator was known and, thus, the case had been "solved."

Site Descriptions

District of Columbia. The MPD has a cold-case unit consisting of 12 homicide investigators and a supervisor. A supervisor in the homicide unit reviews cases at multiple intervals: one day, 15 days, 30 days, and 60 days. In each review, the emphasis is on determining what actions need to be taken by investigators. These could include responding to inquiries by family members, acting on new information, or checking to see whether all leads have been followed up. At the 60-day review, summaries are written for unsolved cases; the summaries incorporate information on witnesses, suspects, and actions taken by investigators. Investigators enter the case into the FBI's VICAP database and check for matches to other local and national cases in the database with a similar modus operandi (MO).

At the MPD, when cases go unsolved for 36 months, they are considered cold. At that point, a formal review is conducted. If there are still leads worth following up, further investigation may be done. But if no good leads are available, a supervisor may decide to close the case administratively with no further action. Of course, cases may be reopened at any time if new information becomes available. Cases are prioritized based on a set of criteria that includes the following:

- whether a suspect has been identified or could potentially be identified through DNA or fingerprint evidence left at the crime scene
- whether eyewitnesses have been identified or a previously uncooperative witness has had a change of heart
- whether potentially probative evidence exists that might be retested with advances in technology.

According to the heads of the unit, new leads on cold cases are often generated from debriefings of individuals arrested for a different crime who have information pertaining to an old case that they wish to trade for consideration on their own case. Another common source of information on cold cases comes from girlfriends of perpetrators who have a falling out with their boyfriends.

When we collected our sample, the MPD was about to open its own crime lab. Historically, the department had relied on the FBI's crime lab to process DNA evidence, but it had grown impatient with the lengthy backlogs to process evidence from cold cases and other evidence not considered top priority. In preparation, graduate students from Marymount University were reviewing cold cases going back to the 1970s and writing summaries to help in prioritizing which should be investigated. The MPD was especially interested to see whether there were cases in which there might be DNA evidence that could be submitted or resubmitted for testing and matching to the CODIS database.

The MPD reported that it reviews 60–70 unsolved cases annually and clears about ten cold cases per year.

Dallas. The Dallas Police Department's (DPD's) cold-case unit was established in 2008; it operates separately from the homicide unit, with four dedicated detectives. The unit is tasked with taking another look at unsolved homicides, of which there are approximately 1,800 in Dallas. The unit looked at 92 issues during 2009; issues include actual reopened cases, as well as inquiries from and meetings with family members and friends of victims. Cold cases are reopened based on one of several occurrences: A family member or friend of the victim comes forward with new, specific information they either had not revealed previously or had recently obtained; a witness contacts the department with new or previously withheld information; or, less frequently, an outside party contacts the department with information regarding an admission of guilt. For example, one case was reopened recently when a woman was attempting to track down her estranged father and had learned from his ex-wife that the father had confessed to his involvement in a murder in Dallas. The woman then contacted DPD detectives, who were able to match the details of the homicide to an open case.

Prisoners, particularly those in federal penitentiaries, also frequently contact the cold-case unit with information about homicides. Although such contacts are not particularly reliable, they have yielded a handful of clearances over the years.

The possibility that evidence gathered in years past can now yield usable DNA due to advances in technology is not by itself a critical factor in opening a cold-case investigation in Dallas. Detectives reported that they do not have the luxury of combing through archives for cases that might have usable DNA evidence. Moreover, DNA from cold cases is not considered a priority by the DNA laboratory.

Many cold cases are cleared by exception, meaning that the case is solved but detectives are unable to make an arrest. Cold cases usually are cleared by exception either because the suspect is deceased or because there is a lack of evidence for prosecution. Occasionally, cases are cleared by exception when a suspect cannot be extradited for prosecution.

Baltimore. The Baltimore Police Cold Case Unit is comprised of two squads, each made up of a sergeant and four detectives. A lieutenant oversees the unit, which has doubled in size since 2009.

The unit does not have a protocol for determining when to initiate a cold-case investigation. According to the head of the homicide division, the most-common situations in which a cold-case investigation begins are (1) when new information is received on a case either from a witness or from a CODIS hit, (2) when detectives working new homicides become overloaded, (3) whey they get Maryland Public Information Act (Md. State Government Code Ann. §10-612) requests (usually made by the Innocence Project), or (4) when new trials are ordered for cases as a result of a successful appeal. Unsolved cases are also reviewed for potential other DNA that can be submitted for laboratory analysis. Cold-case detectives are also responsible for bereavement work—calling surviving family members on the anniversary of murders and responding to family inquiries.

Our observations indicate that the vast majority of cold cases that were worked in Baltimore in particular were the result of statements made by someone attempting to make a deal after being picked up by the police for a crime. Sometimes, such individuals were witnesses to the homicide, but, more often, they had heard someone make an incriminating statement. Either way, their information often gave the police a lead on a suspect that they did not have before. In Baltimore, we saw many exceptional clearances. These often came about when suspects who were about to plead to a federal drug charge gave information on unsolved crimes after being given immunity. Exceptional clearances were also issued when homicide suspects died and witnesses who were unwilling to talk to police earlier gave credible statements about the identity of the killer. Exceptional clearances must be approved by the state's attorney's office.

The Baltimore cold-case unit had 15 clearances in 2009, up from nine the previous year. Those statistics helped to boost the overall clearance rate for homicides, from 48 percent to 55 percent. According to the head of the homicide division, the major reasons that cases are difficult to clear are that many involve killings involving drug deals. (This certainly fits well with our observations: A large majority of homicides included in our case sample stemmed from disputes between young African American males involving drug sales.) These cases nearly always involved shootings in which little physical evidence was left at the scene, other than possibly shell casings. Because there typically was no physical contact between perpetrator and victim, it was rare for the investigators to recover testable DNA evidence that could reveal the identity of the perpetrator. More important is the fact that, in these cases, witnesses typically were also involved in the drug trade, were too afraid of retaliation to talk, or simply distrusted the police.

In fact, Baltimore is where the "no-snitching" culture started (see Young, 2008). It is the result of a homemade DVD that threatened violence against people who reported information about crimes to the police. The idea quickly spread across the country. In response to the video, the Baltimore Police Department created its own campaign, "Keep Talkin'," which used free DVDs and T-shirts.

Denver. The Denver cold-case unit is unique in several respects. First, it receives federal funding for its cold-case work—a $1.5 million federal grant in 2008 that was split between the Denver Police Department, the Office of the Denver District Attorney, and the police department's crime laboratory. The police department and district attorney's office recently received a grant through the Edward Byrne Memorial State and Local Law Enforcement Assistance Grant Program in excess of $900,000 to continue its cold-case work, with a second Byrne grant going to the crime lab. A second unique aspect of cold-case work in Denver is the close partnership forged by the police department and the district attorney's office. The two agencies coordinate efforts in a variety of ways to try to maximize not only the number of cold cases cleared but also the number that result in conviction.

With receipt of the initial funding, the police department and district attorney's office reviewed 4,200 cold-case sexual assaults and homicides to determine whether the cases contained material that could yield potentially testable DNA. The review yielded 1,200 cases with testable DNA samples. When the initial set of 1,200 cases was identified, two assistant district attorneys (ADAs), supported by federal grant funds, worked with the police department to prioritize those cases in which the DNA evidence was most likely to be probative. These were cases with very young or very old victims, cases with extremely violent offenders, homicide cases involving direct contact between victim and perpetrator, cases occurring in inside locations, cases in which the sexual assault or homicide was part of a robbery or burglary, and cases in which the commonly used consent defense could be most easily overcome (i.e., those not involving prostitutes or drug users). At the time of our case study, the 600 highest-priority cases had been processed through the crime lab, and these yielded 103 cases with CODIS hits.

To conduct violent-crime cold-case work efficiently, Denver officials have built on coordination protocols developed in a previous successful cold-case burglary demonstration project also conducted with federal funds. Coordination efforts include training of police investigators by the district attorney's office and crime lab staff on what makes a prosecutable case. The project has also developed protocols for interrogating suspects, for obtaining warrants to obtain suspects' DNA, and for obtaining samples from suspects. Because dealing with victims in sexual-assault cases is a delicate matter, the team includes victims' advocates who notify victims that there has been new movement in their case, keep them apprised of updates, and prepare them for court testimony. The district attorney's office sponsors regular sessions with the head of the crime lab to keep staff abreast of new technology and to give ADAs a chance to ask questions about evidence processing.

When an investigation is initiated on one of the cases with suspect CODIS hits, police detectives work with ADAs to decide whether the case has the potential to overcome a consent defense and to determine what types of evidence will be most important to secure a conviction. Because victim testimony is crucial to rebutting a defense of consent, victims' advocates play a key role. Victims can be hard to locate and, once found, might not be eager to relive painful experiences that they had long ago tried to put behind them. Some victims have had unpleasant experiences with the justice system during the initial investigation and might be reluctant to subject themselves to the possibility of further pain.

Sampling

We set a goal of capturing up to 200 cases that had been actively worked as cold-case investigations per site, or as many as were available. In the three sites where we sampled homicide cases (Washington, Dallas, and Baltimore), we sought equal numbers of cases that had been cleared (whether by arrest or by exceptional means) and cases that had been actively worked but not solved.

We had hoped to use computer databases to draw random samples of cases that were solved and those that were worked on but not solved. However, none of the three homicide case sites had computer files that were suitable for sampling cases. Worse, there was no source that we could use to determine which cases had been worked as cold cases, which had been solved, and which had been worked but not solved. In all three homicide sites, cases in which a cold-case investigation had been conducted were mixed in with other homicide files, with no special notations on the folder that indicated that a cold-case investigation had been undertaken.

Therefore, we were forced to rely on cold-case investigators to sample for us. We asked that they provide us with equal numbers of resolved (cleared either by arrest or through exceptional means) and unresolved cases. In essence, this is a standard case-control sample design: We cannot know whether the cases we received were representative of the entire set of cold-case investigations. However, because the numbers we requested represented a large proportion of cold cases worked at each site, the samples are likely fairly representative of cold-case investigations for each jurisdiction.

In all, we sampled 189 homicide cases in the District of Columbia, 113 in Dallas, and 127 in Baltimore. In each of the homicide sites, roughly half of the cases had been solved, and half remained unsolved. The three sites had different ratios of cases cleared by arrest and exceptional clearances: In Dallas and Baltimore, the great majority of solved cases were cleared by arrest; in the District of Columbia, the ratio of arrests to exceptional clearances was about equal (as shown in Table 3.1).

In Denver, the sampling frame was very different. The Denver sample consisted of all CODIS hits among sexual-assault cases submitted for DNA analysis as part of the jurisdiction's federal grant. In Denver, the research question was not what factors predict success in cold-case investigations; instead, it was what the chance is of obtaining an arrest and conviction given a CODIS hit on suspect DNA.

Table 3.1
Sample Composition, by Site (%)

Disposition of Case	District of Columbia (n = 189)	Dallas (n = 113)	Baltimore (n = 127)	Denver (n = 98)
Cleared by arrest	24	28	35	57
Exceptional clearance	24	13	20	42
Not resolved	51	58	45	1

In the Denver sample, 57 percent of the 98 cases were cleared by arrest, 42 percent were exceptional clearances, and 1 percent remained unresolved at the time of data collection. The meaning of *exceptional clearance* is somewhat different in the Denver sample from its meaning for the other sites, because the Denver sample consisted only of cases in which a CODIS hit had been obtained. Exceptional clearances in Denver were cases that the district attorney felt should not be prosecuted, even though a DNA–suspect match had been made. There were a variety of reasons for which cases might not be filed, including uncooperative or unavailable witnesses, deceased or incarcerated suspects, or DNA evidence that pointed to multiple suspects or was in other ways contradictory. *Unresolved* also had a different meaning for Denver than for the other sites. In Denver, unresolved cases are cases in which the prosecutor had not yet made a determination whether to file.

Case-File Analysis Results

In this section, we discuss our analysis of the case-study file results, starting with an examination of results within selected categories of data across the sites; we then examine significant factors in case clearance and those that predict cold-case success, analyze the Denver sexual-assault case files, and share some on-site observations.

Categories of Data

Using the approach described earlier, we collected seven categories of data from cases sampled in the three homicide sites: victim characteristics, crime context, motivation for crime, human capital, physical evidence, basis for opening the cold-case investigation, and actions taken by cold-case investigators. The data collected for the Denver sample were similar to data collected elsewhere, with some differences resulting from the nature of the crimes. Variables are summarized in Table 3.2, and the analysis for each data category is presented as well.

Victim's Characteristics. Average (mean) ages of the victims did not differ greatly by site. From 33.0 years in Denver to 26.9 in Baltimore, the range was 6.1 years (Table 3.3). Victims were male by an overwhelming majority in the three sites where the samples consisted of homicides, particularly in Baltimore, where 95 percent of the victims were men. In contrast, among Denver's sexual-assault sample, 99 percent of victims were women. In the District of Columbia and in Baltimore, nine in ten victims were black. But both in Dallas and in Denver, whites constituted the largest group of victims, while Hispanics and Asians made up a small percentage of victims in all sites.

We coded whether victims were known to be gang members, drug dealers or users, or prostitutes. Because we do not know how reliably this information was recorded in the investi-

Table 3.2
Data Abstracted from Cold-Case Files

Data Category	Variables
Victim's characteristics	Age, gender, race Known gang member, drug dealer, user, prostitute
Crime context	Time between crime and police arrival Location of body Struggle preceded death Method of death
Motivation	Drug feud Theft Personal or emotional Gang feud Sexual assault
Human capital	Prime suspect identified Prime suspect interviewed Prime suspect arrested and released Eyewitness identified Other witnesses identified
Physical evidence	Weapon recovered Casings recovered Slugs recovered Prints recovered Identified via prints Suspect's DNA tested Suspect identified via DNA
Basis for cold-case investigations	Elapsed time Family inquiry New physical evidence New testing methods or untested evidence Media inquiry New information from witnesses Suspect came forward
Cold-case actions	Tested physical evidence Reinterviewed witnesses Interviewed additional witnesses Identified new theory or suspect Pursued outstanding leads Checked investigative database Conducted lineup

gative case files, we can report only the numbers of victims who were known to fall into these categories; the actual percentages might be significantly higher. Small proportions of victims were known to be gang members, ranging from a high of 13 percent in Baltimore to a low of 3 percent in the District of Columbia.[1] Higher proportions were noted to be drug dealers or users, from one in five to two in five across the sites. The rate of noted drug dealers in Baltimore was roughly twice as high as in the District of Columbia or Dallas. Finally, in all sites, small percentages of victims were noted to be prostitutes. The highest proportion was 9 percent in the Denver sexual-assault sample.

For the Denver sample, we were also able to code an additional factor about the victims, i.e. whether the victim was known to have a criminal history. A surprisingly high number (31 percent) were found to have been arrested on at least one occasion.

[1] We did not capture information about gang affiliation or drug dealing for the Denver sexual-assault sample.

Table 3.3
Victim Characteristics, by Site

Variable	District of Columbia (n = 188)	Dallas (n = 113)	Baltimore (n = 127)	Denver (n = 105)
Age (mean years)	29.4	33.0	26.9	29.3
Gender (%)				
Male	82	74	95	1
Female	18	26	5	99
Race (%)				
Black	90	35	94	11
White	6	43	4	59
Hispanic	3	17	2	14
Asian or other	2	4	0	16
Known gang member (%)				
Yes	3	4	13	—
No	97	96	87	—
Known drug dealer (%)				
Yes	24	20	39	—
No	76	80	61	—
Known drug user (%)				
Yes	30	26	18	22
No	70	74	82	78
Known prostitute (%)				
Yes	3	6	2	9
No	97	94	98	91

Crime Context. Although we would have liked to record the specific time between the homicide or sexual assault and when the police arrived on the scene, this information was not consistently available across the sites. We settled for a dichotomous measure: whether the time to police arrival was less or greater than three hours. In nearly all the Denver cases (93 percent), the time between the assault and police involvement was less than three hours (Table 3.4). Time between death and police arrival on the scene was somewhat greater in the three homicide samples; the police arrived within three hours in 87 percent of the Baltimore cases but in only 62 percent of Dallas cases. We also observed substantial variation in the location of the crime in the different sites. In Dallas, most of the homicides occurred in indoor locations; in the District of Columbia and Baltimore, most deaths occurred on the street, in backyards or alleys, or in other outdoor locations. In Denver, the sexual assaults were evenly split between indoor and outdoor locations.

In all three homicide sites, the most likely cause of death was by firearm. Death by gunshot accounted for 83 percent of cold-case homicides in Baltimore; 78 percent in the District

Table 3.4
Crime Context, by Site (%)

Variable	District of Columbia (n = 188)	Dallas (n = 113)	Baltimore (n = 127)	Denver (n = 105)
Time between crime and police arrival				
Less than three hours	75	62	87	93
More than three hours	25	38	13	7
Location of body (or, in the case of Denver, location of the crime)				
Indoors	20	51	31	44
Outdoors or car	76	49	59	44
Unavailable in file	4	0	10	12
Struggle preceded death				
Yes	16	26	29	—
No	84	74	71	—
Method of death				
Shot	78	62	83	—
Stabbed	12	20	9	—
Strangled	3	12	2	—
Beaten/ bludgeoned	4	2	6	—
Other	3	3	0	—

of Columbia; and 62 percent in Dallas. Stabbings accounted for 10–20 percent of homicides. In at least seven in ten cases in all three homicide samples, there were no indications that death was preceded by a struggle. The method of death in most cases suggests that there was little chance for the perpetrator's DNA to be found at the scene.

For the Denver sexual-assault cases, we were able to collect several additional pieces of information about the crime context. Eighty-eight percent of the Denver assaults were perpetrated by a lone individual, and 12 percent by multiple perpetrators. In a large majority of cases (85 percent), that individual was a stranger to the victim. In a majority of cases (58 percent), a gun, knife, or other weapon was used to intimidate the victim into submission. Five percent of the victims suffered broken bones, and 48 percent suffered bruises or scratches, while 47 percent of the victims had no visible injuries.

Motivation. For the three homicide samples, we gathered information, when available, about investigators' beliefs about the motivation for the crime. In many cases, more than one motivation was suggested, so the categories in Table 3.5 are not mutually exclusive. The most-common motivations for homicides were personal or emotional disputes (present in 58 percent of Dallas cold cases, 28 percent of District of Columbia cold cases, and 32 percent of Baltimore cold cases) or conflicts arising from drug sales (present in 30 percent of Baltimore cold cases, 27 percent of Dallas cold cases, and 15 percent of District of Columbia cold cases), and theft

Table 3.5
Suspected Motivation, by Site (%)

Variable	District of Columbia (n = 188)	Dallas (n = 113)	Baltimore (n = 127)
Drug feud			
Yes	15	27	30
No	85	73	70
Theft			
Yes	32	29	18
No	68	71	82
Personal/emotional			
Yes	38	58	32
No	62	42	68
Gang feud (%)			
Yes	2	4	9
No	98	96	91
Sexual assault			
Yes	4	14	2
No	96	86	98

NOTE: Denver is excluded from this table because the motivation categories for homicides do not fit sexual-assault cases.

(present in 18 percent of Baltimore cold cases, 29 percent of Dallas cold cases, and 32 percent of District of Columbia cold cases). Investigators ascribed gang feuds and sexual assaults as motives in a small proportion of homicides. Still, it is noteworthy that, although sexual assault was ascribed as a motivation in fewer than 5 percent of homicides in the District of Columbia and Baltimore, it was thought to be a factor in 14 percent of Dallas cold-case homicides.

Human Capital. For each of the study sites, we coded information on human capital based on information about suspects, eyewitnesses, and other witnesses. In at least one-third of the homicide cold cases at each site, a prime suspect had been identified in the original investigation, ranging from 32 percent in Baltimore to 50 percent in the District of Columbia. The situation was very different in the Denver sexual-assault sample, in which a prime suspect had been identified in 17 percent of the cold cases (Table 3.6). Only Dallas had interviewed a prime suspect in a significant proportion (30 percent) of cases. In the other sites, investigators interviewed a prime suspect in fewer than 15 percent of the sampled cases. In even fewer cases, a suspect had been arrested but released in the initial investigation. Again, this occurred in a significant proportion of cases in Dallas (where an arrest had been made in the initial investigation in 13 percent of cases) and in fewer than 5 percent of cases in the other three sites.

In all three homicide samples, an eyewitness had been identified in roughly half the initial investigations. Not surprisingly, eyewitnesses had been identified in the initial investigation in 15 percent of the Denver sexual-assault sample. In all sites, other witnesses had been

Table 3.6
Human Capital, by Site (%)

Variable	District of Columbia (n = 188)	Dallas (n = 113)	Baltimore (n = 127)	Denver (n = 105)
Prime suspect identified				
Yes	50	49	32	17
No	50	51	68	81
Prime suspect interviewed				
Yes	13	30	11	8
No	87	70	89	92
Prime suspect arrested, released				
Yes	3	13	1	3
No	97	87	99	97
Eyewitness identified				
Yes	57	48	43	15
No	43	52	57	85
Other witnesses identified				
Yes	90	58	72	52
No	10	42	28	48

identified in the initial investigations, ranging from 52 percent among cases in the Denver sexual-assault sample to fully 90 percent in the District of Columbia sample.

Victims' willingness to cooperate is a key factor in arresting and prosecuting perpetrators. DNA or other physical evidence is not dispositive in sexual-assault cases because the defense often admits that there was sexual contact but contends that the contact was consensual. In the Denver sexual-assault sample, investigators noted that victims were cooperative in 67 percent of the cases, somewhat cooperative in 20 percent of the cases, and uncooperative in 13 percent of the cases.

Physical Evidence. Because most homicides were committed using guns, it is not surprising that police recovered weapons in a small proportion of cases (Table 3.7). Guns, after all, are easy to transport and conceal. Recovery of a weapon was noted to be as high as 20 percent in initial investigations in Dallas and as low as 2 percent of cases in Denver (where weapons were used in only half of the sexual-assault cases). Slugs and casings were collected in half to three-quarters of initial investigations in all three homicide sites. Fingerprints were lifted in half of the cases in the District of Columbia and Dallas but in less than 10 percent of the cases in the Baltimore and Denver samples. However, prints led to identification of suspects in only a small percentage of cases, ranging from a low of 2 percent in Baltimore to a high of 12 percent in Dallas and the District of Columbia.

Potential suspect DNA was found and tested in 12–22 percent of initial investigations in the three homicide samples but in half of the initial investigations of Denver sexual-assault cases. Suspects were identified through DNA matches in 1–8 percent of the four samples.

Table 3.7
Physical Evidence, by Site (%)

Variable	District of Columbia (n = 188)	Dallas (n = 113)	Baltimore (n = 127)	Denver (n = 105)
Weapon recovered				
Yes	7	20	12	2
No	93	80	88	98
Casings recovered				
Yes	59	43	56	—
No	41	57	44	—
Slugs removed				
Yes	66	53	74	—
No	34	47	26	—
Prints recovered				
Yes	54	50	11	9
No	46	50	89	91
Identification through prints				
Yes	12	12	2	7
No	88	88	98	93
Suspect DNA tested				
Yes	12	15	22	51
No	88	85	78	49
Suspect identified via DNA				
Yes	1	4	8	1
No	99	96	92	99

Basis for Opening Cold-Case Investigations. The most-common reasons for opening cold-case investigations varied by site (Table 3.8). In the District of Columbia, about half of all cold-case investigations were initiated as a result of policies that called for reviews of unsolved cases based on elapsed time. In Dallas, family inquiries were the determining factor in opening more than one in three cold-case investigations; in the other sites, family inquiries were rarely cause for opening an investigation. In Baltimore, new information from witnesses accounted for more than half of all cold-case investigations. According to what we observed in case files, most of these cases were reopened as the result of an interrogation or arrest of an individual who was willing to give information about a past crime he or she witnessed or about which he or she had key information in exchange for consideration on the charge he or she was facing. In Denver, untested physical evidence or new testing methods (DNA) were key in close to half of all cold-case investigations in our sample. This would be expected because we included in our Denver sample all cases in which previously untested DNA evidence was processed using federal grant funds.

Table 3.8
Basis for Opening a Cold-Case Investigation, by Site (%)

Variable	District of Columbia (n = 188)	Dallas (n = 113)	Baltimore (n = 127)	Denver (n = 105)
Elapsed time				
Yes	52	1	17	49
No	48	99	83	51
Family inquiry				
Yes	15	37	7	1
No	85	63	93	99
New physical evidence				
Yes	5	10	12	42
No	95	90	88	58
New testing methods or untested evidence				
Yes	0	1	0	8
No	100	99	100	92
Media inquiry				
Yes	0	0	0	0
No	100	100	100	100
New information from witnesses				
Yes	16	14	58	2
No	84	86	42	98
Suspect came forward				
Yes	3	0	3	—
No	97	100	97	—
Information from another case				
Yes	2	0	1	—
No	98	100	99	—
Other reasons[a]				
Yes	4	0	13	—
No	96	100	87	—

[a] Includes delayed CODIS hits on DNA material, inquiries by the U.S. Attorney's Office, information passed along by federal investigators, and arrest of a prime suspect for a similar crime.

Some of the potential motivations for opening cold-case investigations that we thought would be common proved to be quite rare in all the sites. Information gained in another case (for example, a DNA link to an identified suspect in another crime, suspects coming forward, and new physical evidence) was stated to be the reason for opening 10 percent or fewer of the cold-case investigations at each site. We did not encounter a single case at any of the sites in which a cold-case investigation was initiated as a result of a media inquiry.

Actions Taken by Cold-Case Investigators

In Table 3.9, we review the actions taken during cold-case investigations (multiple answers were coded when applicable). Again, the actions were idiosyncratic by site. In Denver, of course, the main action taken—in three of four cases—was to test DNA evidence. Testing physical evidence was an action taken in, at best, one in four cases among the three homicide cold-case

Table 3.9
Cold-Case Investigators' Actions, by Site (%)

Variable	District of Columbia (n = 188)	Dallas (n = 113)	Baltimore (n = 127)	Denver (n = 105)
Tested physical evidence				
Yes	22	27	13	73
No	78	73	87	27
Reinterviewed witnesses				
Yes	42	27	39	69
No	58	73	61	31
Interviewed additional witnesses				
Yes	31	30	67	5
No	69	70	33	95
Identified new theory or suspect				
Yes	14	12	10	76
No	86	88	90	24
Pursued outstanding leads				
Yes	26	26	20	2
No	74	74	80	98
Checked investigative database				
Yes	49	9	6	2
No	51	91	94	98
Conducted lineup				
Yes	0	0	32	—
No	100	100	68	—
Ran criminal checks on suspects				
Yes	0	17	0	58
No	100	83	100	42

samples. Three in four of the Denver sexual-assault cold-case investigations involved pursuing a new theory or suspect based on results of the DNA testing, compared with just about 10 percent of cases in the other three sites. More than two in three cold-case investigations in Denver also involved reinterviewing witnesses. Although this was also a common activity in cold-case investigations in the other sites, it was not done in more than half of the homicide investigations. Denver was the only one of the sites to run criminal checks on suspects in a majority of cold cases, presumably those individuals identified through DNA testing in the cold-case investigations.

Interviewing additional witnesses was noted in more than two in three of the cold-case investigations in Baltimore. As stated earlier, these were mostly individuals picked up for other crimes who wanted to make a deal with the prosecution. Baltimore was the only site to make frequent use of suspect lineups. In half the investigations in the District of Columbia, detectives checked information in investigative databases. Finally, cold-case investigators noted pursuing outstanding leads from the original investigation in about one-quarter of the three homicide samples.

Significant Factors in Case Clearance

In Table 3.10, we present the factors cited in case files as being instrumental to case clearance. We found that, among the three sites with homicide cases, new information from witnesses or information from new witnesses was the most prevalent reason cited for case clearance. This was true for nearly two in three cases cleared in the District of Columbia and Baltimore and for nearly half the cases cleared in Dallas. In contrast, the most common reason given for clearing cases in Denver was a hit from DNA samples, cited in 75 percent of cases cleared. (In the other three sites, DNA hits accounted for no more than one in ten cleared cases.)

Information from informants was cited in 14 percent of case clearances in the District of Columbia and in 12 percent of clearances in Baltimore. Confessions elicited from perpetrators accounted for more than one in ten clearances only in Baltimore, where it was common for defendants to plead to outstanding state charges as part of a federal plea deal on drug conspiracy charges. Physical evidence or a link to other crimes was cited by more than one in ten cases only in the District of Columbia.

Predicting Cold-Case Success

Combining data from the three homicide samples (Baltimore, Washington, and Dallas), we attempted to determine whether it was possible to predict which cases were likely to be resolved based on information about the victim, crime context, motivation, evidence, basis for opening the cold-case investigation, and actions taken by cold-case investigators. The goal of this analysis was to find the variables that were associated with the probability of solving a cold case. Thus, the dependent variable was whether the case was solved or not, i.e., whether the case was cleared by an arrest or resulted in an exceptional clearance.

We investigated 45 variables of interest through four models by categorizing the variables into groups based on when they occurred in the investigation.[2] The variables in the data set were divided into four categories based on temporal sequence: crime context, initial investi-

---

[2] Because the dependent measure is binary (cleared or not cleared), logistic regression was the most appropriate multivariate approach. Because we have three different sites, the assumption homoscedastic standard errors might not hold, and observations within a site might not be independent. To account for differences in standard errors across the three sites,

Table 3.10
Significant Factors in Case Clearance, by Site (%)

Significant Factors	District of Columbia (n = 188)	Dallas (n = 113)	Baltimore (n = 127)	Denver (n = 82)
Information from witnesses				
Yes	63	47	61	1
No	37	53	39	99
Information from informants				
Yes	14	6	12	0
No	86	94	88	100
DNA match				
Yes	3	9	10	75
No	97	91	90	25
Perpetrator statements				
Yes	2	2	12	0
No	98	98	88	100
Physical evidence				
Yes	13	9	6	1
No	87	91	94	99
Link to other crime				
Yes	11	2	0	0
No	89	98	100	100

gation results, basis for opening cold case, and cold-case investigator actions. Five variables from the original database were not included in the model because they had very little or no variation. They were Basis New Testing, Basis Media, Basis Suspect, Basis Other Case, and Actions—Convene Grand Jury.

Results of the logistic regression procedure are presented in Table 3.11. Because we used a logistic regression, the log-odds ratio was reported. The log-odds ratio is a measure of the effect size and describes the strength of association of the two binary data values. In our case, it identifies the odds of solving a cold case if we hold all other values constant. For example, the odds of the case being solved when the victim was found in a private residence are 1.631 times as large as the odds when the victim was found elsewhere, holding all other values constant. Odd ratios close to 1 imply that there is no change due to the predictor variable.

The results indicate that three crime context variables significant at the 5-percent level or less are associated with case clearance (model 1). Specifically, the chance of solving a case declines with increasing age of the case and when victims are known to be drug users. Then again, finding the victim in a private residence increases the odds of solving the case.

---

the errors were clustered by site, and the robust standard errors are reported. This procedure acts to minimize intrasite correlation.

Table 3.11
Multivariate Modeling of Cold-Case Clearance

Variable	Model 1	Model 2	Model 3	Model 4
Black	0.189 (0.166)*	0.239 (0.296)	0.338 (0.381)	0.306 (0.347)
White	0.226 (0.177)*	0.282 (0.399)	0.273 (0.307)	0.196 (0.221)
Hispanic	0.440 (0.394)	0.294 (0.453)	0.362 (0.484)	0.304 (.397)
Gender	0.858 (0.147)	1.187 (0.412)	1.266 (0.147)**	1.645 (0.323)**
Age	0.998 (0.006)	0.979 (0.005)***	0.982 (0.008)**	0.979 (0.009)**
Drug user	0.456 (0.063)***	0.380 (0.079)***	0.396 (0.103)***	0.355 (0.135)***
Gang member	1.148 (0.748)	0.848 (0.961)	1.302 (1.773)	1.065 (1.606)
Drug dealer	1.300 (0.186)*	1.319 (0.283)	1.179 (0.418)	1.094 (0.196)
Prostitute	2.202 (2.845)	1.451 (2.748)	1.188 (2.216)	0.965 (2.064)
Found: outside	1.162 (0.292)	1.273 (0.697)	1.446 (0.702)	1.375 (0.701)
Found: private residence	1.631 (0.301)***	2.692 (1.491)*	3.154 (1.722)**	3.013 (2.325)
Recovery time	1.124 (0.251)	1.273 (0.226)	1.465 (0.086)***	1.534 (0.281)**
Struggle	0.869 (0.175)	0.576 (0.158)**	0.431 (0.116)***	0.458 (0.139)**
Method of death	1.413 (0.484)	1.135 (0.399)	1.277 (0.819)	1.328 (0.924)
Age of case	0.992 (0.003)**	0.991 (0.004)**	0.993 (0.004)*	0.994 (0.003)*
Motivation known		6.539 (1.902)***	6.858 (3.567)***	8.732 (4.318)***
Drug feud		1.112 (0.460)	1.166 (0.346)	1.132 (0.492)
Theft		0.916 (0.242)	1.043 (0.356)	1.067 (0.320)
Personal emotional		0.679 (0.172)	0.580 (0.080)***	0.575 (0.055)***
Gang feud		0.792 (0.839)	0.381 (0.653)	0.327 (0.568)
Sexual assault		0.660 (0.733)	0.772 (0.727)	0.978 (1.001)
Prime suspect		4.183 (1.725)***	4.178 (2.072)***	4.296 (2.221)***
Prime suspect interviewed		0.675 (0.586)	0.826 (0.693)	0.862 (0.812)
Arrested		0.897 (0.350)	0.523 (0.083)***	0.623 (0.052)***
Eyewitness		1.085 (0.208)	1.002 (0.272)	1.036 (0.351)
Other witness		0.701 (0.031)***	1.008 (0.090)	1.071 (0.178)
Weapon recovered		0.916 (0.797)	0.933 (0.956)	0.930 (0.853)
Shells recovered		0.896 (0.159)	0.786 (0.154)	0.767 (0.153)
Slugs removed		0.791 (0.301)	0.748 (0.412)	0.684 (0.429)
Prints recovered		0.681 (0.178)	0.790 (0.183)	0.836 (0.200)
Identification made		1.206 (0.831)	0.964 (0.394)	0.935 (0.405)
Suspect DNA tested		1.808 (1.268)	1.859 (1.269)	1.967 (1.447)

Table 3.11—Continued

Variable	Model 1	Model 2	Model 3	Model 4
Suspect DNA identified		3.225 (5.576)	2.840 (5.824)	3.157 (7.005)
Basis: routine			0.183 (0.114)***	0.160 (0.125)**
Basis: family			0.096 (0.045)***	0.093 (0.050)***
Basis: physical information			0.827 (0.294)	0.594 (0.171)*
Basis: new witness information			0.696 (0.192)	0.416 (0.252)
Basis: other			1.088 (1.404)	0.854 (1.342)
Actions: tested				1.229 (0.249)
Actions: reinterviewed witness				1.026 (0.420)
Actions: new theory				2.188 (0.469)***
Actions: leads				1.325 (0.394)
Actions: additional witness				2.039 (0.903)
Actions: background				1.051 (0.259)
Actions: lineup				4.139 (2.468)**
Pseudo R-squared	0.0915	0.2815	0.3528	0.3862

NOTE: Numbers in parentheses are robust standard errors. * = statistically significant at the 10-percent level. ** = statistically significant at the 5-percent level. *** = statistically significant at the 1-percent level.

When we introduce variables associated with the initial investigation, the explanatory power is increased (model 2). Four crime context variables—gender, age, location of the body, and struggle—become important predictors in model 2. Cases were more likely to be solved if they involved younger or male victims and if the victim's body was found indoors at a private residence. Surprisingly, cases were less likely to be solved if a struggle preceded death. Progress made during the initial investigation was also associated with the success of cold-case investigations. If a motive is discovered during the initial investigation, if the motive proved to involve a personal feud, or if a prime suspect is identified, the odds of a successful cold-case investigation improve.

In model 3, we introduced variables associated with the motivation for initiating a cold-case investigation. The two motivational variables that proved to bear a significant relationship to cold-case clearance were opening a cold-case investigation based on victim's family inquiry or opening the investigation based on elapsed time alone. The odds ratios indicate that, when cases are initiated for either of these reasons, the likelihood of a successful resolution is lower, most likely because there is no evidentiary basis for initiating an investigation.

Finally, in model 4, we introduce the final set of variables—the actions taken during the cold-case investigation. The model indicates that the chances of solving a case increase when investigators develop a new theory of the motivation for the crime or conduct a suspect lineup.

Table 3.12 is provided to help the reader understand the direction of the relationships and includes only significant variables. All told, the full model (model 4) accounts for 39 percent of variation in whether cold cases are solved, as shown at the bottom of Table 3.11.

Analysis of Denver Sexual-Assault Cases

In Denver, where the sample consisted of all cases in which a suspect DNA sample had been submitted for laboratory analysis and a match was found, the research question was whether having a match would lead to arrests, filings, and convictions. There are many reasons that a conviction might not be possible, even with a suspect DNA match: Victim/witnesses might be uncooperative or their testimony unreliable with the passage of time; suspects or victim/

Table 3.12
Coding of Statistically Significant Predictor Variables

Variable	Explanation
Black	1 if the victim was black; 0 otherwise
White	1 if the victim was white; 0 otherwise
Gender	1 if the victim was male; 0 if the victim was female
Age	Age of the victim
Drug user	1 if the victim was a drug user; 0 otherwise
Drug dealer	1 if the victim was a drug dealer; 0 otherwise
Found: private residence	1 if the victim was found in a private residence; 0 otherwise
Recovery time	1 if time elapsed before victim found; 0 if victim found immediately
Struggle	1 if a struggle preceded death; 0 otherwise
Age of case	Age of the case in months
Motivation known	1 if the motivation is known; 0 otherwise
Personal emotional	1 if the case was likely personal or emotional; 0 otherwise
Prime suspect	1 if there is a prime suspect ; 0 otherwise
Prime suspect arrested and released	1 if an arrest was made; 0 otherwise
Suspect DNA tested	1 if the suspect's DNA has been tested; 0 otherwise
Prints recovered	1 if prints were recovered; 0 otherwise
Other witness	1 if there was another witness; 0 otherwise
Suspect DNA identified	1 if the suspect's DNA has been identified ; 0 otherwise
Basis: routine	1 if the basis for reopening the case was routine ; 0 otherwise
Basis: family	1 if the family was the reason for reopening the case; 0 otherwise
Basis: physical information	1 if the basis for reopening the case was new physical evidence; 0 otherwise
Actions: lineup	1 if a new lineup was conducted; 0 otherwise
Actions: additional witness	1 if additional witnesses were interviewed; 0 otherwise
Actions: new theory	1 if a new theory was developed; 0 otherwise

witnesses might be unavailable; or the DNA match might be inconclusive because it pointed to a consensual partner or only to another crime scene but not a suspect.

Of 97 DNA-match cases for which we have information, 56, or nearly six in ten, resulted in an arrest and 55 in a court filing. In the other 42 cases, the district attorney decided that there was not a strong enough case to file. As Table 3.13 demonstrates, there were two primary reasons for not filing cases. Victim or witness problems were the stated causes for not filing in 43 percent of the cases declined by the prosecutor. The other frequent reason given by prosecutors for not filing was that the DNA match did not yield a suspect but instead pointed to another crime.

Fully 93 percent of those cases that were filed resulted in convictions (Table 3.14), either by pleas or by a verdict at trial. Just 6 percent of filings were dismissed, and 2 percent of defendants were found not guilty after trial. Moreover, a large majority of those who were convicted received lengthy prison terms. In fact, 56 percent of those convicted were sentenced to 25-year or longer sentences.

The Denver data allow us to ask a different policy question from what we were able to ask at the other sites. In Denver, we know that, even when a CODIS hit is obtained, there is still a good likelihood that the prosecutor will not file a case, or—in some cases—might not win a conviction once a case is filed. Therefore, the question of interest is, "Given a suspect match

Table 3.13
Reasons Given by Prosecutor for Declining Cases with DNA Matches (n = 42)

Reason	Percentage
DNA match is to another crime, not to a suspect	38
Victim/witness uncooperative or testimony judged unreliable	36
Victim/witness unavailable	7
Suspect deceased or in prison	5
DNA match is to consensual partner	5
No specific reason given by prosecutor	12

NOTE: Percentages do not sum to 100 percent because of rounding.

Table 3.14
Dispositions of Cases Filed by Prosecutor in Cases with a Suspect DNA Match (n = 52)

Disposition	Percentage
Pled guilty	56
Convicted after trial	37
Dismissed	6
Found not guilty at trial	2

NOTE: Percentages do not sum to 100 percent because of rounding. The table excludes four cases pending at the time of data collection.

from CODIS, what information that is available when a cold-case investigation is opened predicts whether a case will result in conviction?" To answer that question, we conducted an analysis of the Denver cases, including only those cases in which a match was made directly to a suspect.

We followed a logistic regression procedure similar to that used in the analysis of the three homicide sites. Variables in the database that had a lot of missing observations or no variation among observations were not used in the model. Three variables (race, visible injuries, and coercion) were not used because of missing observations, and the variable "Elapsed Time" was not used because there was no variation in the variable. The results of the analysis are presented in Table 3.15.

The odds of obtaining a conviction increase in cases with a victim who has expressed willingness to cooperate with authorities and in cases in which the victim does not have a criminal record. These findings make sense: Sexual-assault cases are extremely difficult to prosecute without a willing and credible victim because the issue is not just whether sex occurred but also whether the victim consented. Together, the variables in the model explain nearly 40 percent of the variation in convictions.

Observations While on Site

In analyzing the survey data and spending time on site, we made some interesting observations about how cold-case work is conducted. The first observation, and one that surprised us, is that cold-case work is usually opportunistic. We had expected that agencies would routinely assess unsolved cases for cold-case investigation potential, would study the case and actions taken to date, undertake some preliminary investigative steps, and then determine whether a full-fledged cold-case investigation was called for.

Instead, what we most often found was that cold-case investigations were the result of breaks in the case. Most often, the police would pick up someone on some charge after a case went cold, and the suspect on the new case would offer to trade information about the cold case in exchange for favorable treatment on the new charge. Or a girlfriend might break up with the (unknown) perpetrator in a cold case and suddenly be willing to testify against her former boyfriend. Or a suspect might be arrested on federal charges and, as part of a plea bargain, confess to a local cold-case charge. In any of these situations, a cold-case investigation would be opened. But, in reality, when the investigation was opened, the case had essentially been solved.

We also heard in our conversations with two cold-case investigators at different sites that cold-case investigations were sometimes undertaken when agencies needed to "plus up" their clearance rates. If the end of a reporting cycle was approaching and the homicide clearance rate appeared lower than what an agency was comfortable reporting, homicide investigators were assigned to review cold cases to determine whether some might be easily solved to bolster the number of cases cleared during that time period. Because clearance rates are based on the number of cases cleared during a specific time period divided by the number of new cases during the period, adding in older solved cases is an effective way to inflate a clearance rate that might otherwise appear anemic. At least one other researcher has made a similar observation (Davies, 2004, p. 197).

Our observations also suggested that agencies know little about the efficiency of cold-case work. Our experience has suggested that agencies do not track even the most-rudimentary statistics on the number of cold-case investigations opened, the number cleared, the number that

Table 3.15
Logistic Regression Predicting Convictions Among Sexual-Assault Cases in Which a CODIS Suspect Match Was Obtained

Variable	Odds of Conviction
Crime context	
Criminal history	0.068 (0.057)***
Age	1.004 (0.028)
Drug or alcohol	0.418 (0.419)
Sex worker	0.501 (1.550)
Initial investigation results	
Crime location	1.410 (1.066)
Perpetrators	0.667 (0.744)
Relationship	4.593 (5.483)
Cooperation	5.474 (4.313)**
Property taken	1.822 (1.661)
Suspect identified	0.810 (0.855)
Person of Interest identified	0.131 (0.219)
Eyewitness	1.603 (1.865)
Bystanders present	0.238 (0.270)
Other witness	1.405 (1.115)
MO match	8.171 (17.848)
Suspect match	5.154 (10.102)
Case age	0.991 (0.009)
Pseudo R^2	0.3693
Probability > chi^2	0.005

NOTE: Numbers in parentheses are robust standard errors. * = statistically significant at the 10-percent level. ** = statistically significant at the 5-percent level. *** = statistically significant at the 1-percent level.

result in an arrest, or hours spent on cold-case investigations. Moreover, according to survey respondents, the rate of success in cold-case investigations is low: One in five cold cases results in a clearance, and this includes not just arrests but also exceptional clearances. Thus, although it is true that solving an old case might be very satisfying to investigators and might give the victim's family some peace, the question remains, "At what cost?" Without better documentation of cold-case statistics, we cannot determine whether the expenditure of time and resources justifies the ultimate payoff.

We have also noted in our time on site that there generally is no tracking of what happens to cases after they are cleared. That is, outcome information generally stops at the point of clearance, whether by arrest or by exceptional means. The cold-case units did not track whether cases that were cleared were also prosecuted and convicted. Many of the clearances in our sample were exceptional clearances—that is, they did not result in an arrest because the suspect was dead, was serving a lengthy prison sentence, was recently convicted on federal charges, or simply could not be found. Moreover, there is no reason to think from the survey data and from our conversations with investigators that, even in cases in which an arrest is made, a successful prosecution is by any means guaranteed. Witnesses might have disappeared or died, or memories might have clouded over time. Physical evidence might be lost or might have deteriorated.

Denver, where police and prosecutors work hand-in-hand from the beginning of cold-case investigations, was a striking exception. Because the prosecutor's office is involved, for Denver, we have good data on case outcomes beyond the point of clearance. But, even with the cooperative arrangement between police and the district attorney in Denver, there still are many cases in which a successful prosecution is not possible despite the fact that a DNA match has been made. One out of every three cases in which a DNA suspect match had been made were not prosecuted for a variety of reasons, including uncooperative, unreliable, or unavailable witnesses; a deceased or incarcerated suspect; or DNA evidence that pointed to multiple suspects or was in other ways contradictory.

Summary

Working with each of the four sites, we reviewed up to 200 case files of solved and unsolved cases that have been assigned to cold-case squads and extracted attributes of the crime and attributes of the investigation that affected cold-case solvability. Based on that examination, the following key findings emerged:

- One can identify factors that predict whether cold-case investigations will be successful, including the basis for initiating the cold-case investigation (e.g., family pressure, simple passage of time since crime occurred); characteristics of the victim and crime (e.g., age of case, location of body, victim age and gender, victim known to be a drug user); progress made during the initial investigation (e.g., known motivation for the crime, identification of a suspect during the initial investigation); and actions of cold-case investigators (e.g., developing a new theory of the crime and suspect motivation and conducting lineups).
- Clearing a cold case does not automatically lead to making an arrest. A substantial portion of successful investigations in all sites (from one in three to one in two) did not result in an arrest for a variety of reasons, including inability to locate witnesses, uncooperative witnesses, suspect who is deceased or incarcerated, or DNA results that implicated multiple individuals or were otherwise inconclusive.
- In sexual-assault cold cases, even when a suspect DNA match has been made, about one-third of cases are not filed because of problems with victim cooperation, credibility, or availability of suspects who are deceased or in prison. However, those cases that are prosecuted resulted in convictions and lengthy prison terms more than 90 percent of the time.
- Cooperation between police and prosecutors can improve both the efficiency and effectiveness of cold-case investigations. Typically, prosecutors are not brought into the picture until cold-case investigations have produced results. But, when police consult with prosecutors beginning at case screening, as is the case in Denver, prosecutors can offer

advice on whether the case is likely to produce a conviction if cleared and on what kinds of evidence will be most compelling in court.

CHAPTER FOUR

Conclusions and Recommendations

In this chapter, we provide an overview of some of the key conclusions and offer some recommendations going forward.

Conclusions

In answering the two study questions, we made use of a national law enforcement survey and an analysis of cold cases from four sites identified in the survey. Here, we first summarize some of the key findings from both sets of analyses and then some more-general findings.

Key Findings from the National Law Enforcement Cold-Case Survey

The law enforcement survey revealed information about how cold-case investigations are organized and funded. One of the major findings was that cold-case investigations are mostly opportunistic. Only a small minority of agencies responding indicated that they had a protocol governing the initiation of a cold-case investigation. One in ten respondents worked for agencies that had dedicated cold-case investigators, and 7 percent had a dedicated cold-case unit. Instead of assessing unsolved cases to determine their suitability for being designated a cold case, the more common pattern is to wait until someone with inside knowledge of a crime comes forward; these individuals are generally motivated by a score to settle or consideration on a new charge. At that point, a cold-case investigation is opened. Systematic screening of cases for their investigative potential is most likely to occur when homicide units are looking for ways to increase their clearance rates by identifying cold cases that can be cleared exceptionally.

Federal funding might help to make cold-case work more systematic. Some jurisdictions have received grants for laboratory testing of DNA material in old cases, so, in these agencies, comprehensive screening is becoming more common. Because the survey indicated that just one in five agencies funds cold-case work out of its regular budget and cold-case DNA work has become a U.S. Department of Justice priority, federal funding is essential if this activity is to be expanded and organized.

We also found that most cold-case investigations involve homicides. Cold-case murder investigations outnumber other types of cold-case investigations by at least two to one in our survey results. Two in three agencies responding to the survey had conducted at least one cold-case homicide investigation during the past year, compared with one in three that had conducted missing-person cold-case investigations and smaller proportions that had conducted cold-case investigations for sex offenses, burglaries, robberies, or other crimes.

According to survey respondents, clearance rates for cold-case investigations are low. Dividing the number of cold cases worked during the past year by the number cleared yields an average clearance rate of one in five, or around 20 percent. Higher clearance rates were associated with agencies having budgets for cold-case work and with investigators having access to investigative databases. We were surprised that survey data indicated that, based on respondent estimates, just one in 20 cold-case investigations with a known perpetrator resulted in arrest and just one in 100 resulted in conviction. Of course, the survey responses were based on estimates, and we have no way of knowing how accurate those estimates were. From our experience on site and the lack of statistics kept on cold-case investigations, we believe that the estimates are highly unreliable. Still, they do raise questions about the efficiency of cold-case work.

Key Findings from the Case Site Analysis

The analysis of homicide cases in three sites yielded information about cases and actions likely to result in successful cold-case outcomes. The basis for opening cases was associated with success of cold-case investigations: Cases were less likely to be cleared if the cold-case investigation were initiated because of family pressure or triggered simply by the passage of time. Some factors associated with crime context—whether the victim was a drug user and age of the case—were associated with clearances: A case was more likely to be solved if it was more recent, if it did not involve a drug user, and if the victim had been found in a private residence. It was more likely to be solved if the victim was younger or male. Also, some factors associated with the initial investigation—whether there was a known motivation for the crime and whether a prime suspect had been identified—also predicted success: A case in which the initial investigation had yielded this information was more likely to result in a successful cold-case outcome than a case in which fewer insights were available to start the cold-case investigation. Actions taken by cold-case investigators—developing a new theory of the crime and suspect lineups—were also associated with cold-case clearance.

Our analyses can help us determine associations but not causal relationships. Especially with actions taken by cold-case investigators, we cannot be sure whether those actions helped bring about successful resolutions or whether they are simply markers for cases that had already been solved. We do know that it is common to start a cold-case file at the point that a new witness comes forward (often in trying to make a deal for lenient treatment on a recent charge). In such cases, it is not the act of investigators in interviewing the witness that "solves" the case but rather an unsolicited action on the part of the individual providing the new information. Similarly, suspect lineups are likely not factors that lead to solving a case as often as they are an indicator that investigators already have the case figured out.

The findings from the Denver sample of sexual-assault CODIS hits addressed a different policy question: What is the likelihood of an arrest and conviction in cases in which a DNA match has been made? We found that about one-third of the cases in which a match to a suspect had been made were dropped, primarily because of problems with victim cooperation, credibility, or availability. In sexual-assault cases, in which a defense of consent can be offered, testimony from a credible, cooperative victim is very important. Once the decision to file a case was made, more than nine in ten filings resulted in a convictions and lengthy prison terms.

The Denver sample also highlights the importance of cooperation between police and prosecutors. In Denver, prosecutors are consulted as soon as a cold-case investigation is contemplated. Prosecutors can offer advice on whether the case is likely to produce a conviction if cleared and on what kinds of evidence will be most compelling in court. This kind of consultation is most important in sexual-assault cases, in which DNA evidence is seldom, by itself, dispositive.

Other Overarching Conclusions

According to this research, there are three types of cold-case investigations. The three types involve very different processes and, if we are to come to understand the value of cold-case investigations, we need to draw a clear distinction between them and to develop separate estimates of their costs and benefits. The first type is the classic cold-case investigation, in which a detective picks up a case file because of a family or media inquiry or during a procedural review of cases that have remained unsolved for a specified length of time. The investigator reviews the file and determines whether there are leads that have not been thoroughly exploited. For example, are there potential witnesses who were not interviewed or whose story seems inconsistent in light of other evidence? This type of case is typified by work of the Vidocq Society, a group of forensic professionals and motivated private citizens who, as a public service, donate deductive, scientific, and other talents to solve cold cases for which local law enforcement has requested their help. These are the least common types of cold-case investigations.

The second type of cold-case investigation is that based on availability of forensic tests. Forensic material from old cases once thought not to be amenable to DNA testing might now be testable thanks to advances in DNA technology. DNA samples that could once be matched only to DNA samples from one or two known suspects can be run against the CODIS database, which contains information on the DNA of tens of thousands of offenders. A DNA match is then the basis for a potentially strong case against the suspect. Federal funds are making this type of cold-case investigation increasingly common.

The third type of cold-case investigation consists of those cases opened only because an individual charged with a crime confesses to the outstanding crime as part of a plea deal or because an eyewitness announces a willingness to finger a suspect in return for leniency after the witness is arrested for participating in a crime.

Each of these types of investigations has implications for cost and for the likelihood of success. The third type of case involves little new investigation, and the cost is low. If the criterion for success is clearance, all such cases result in at least an exceptional clearance, and a large majority are also likely to result in conviction. Submitting or resubmitting DNA material for laboratory testing (the second type of case) is relatively inexpensive (the initial investment is the cost of DNA laboratory processing), but the rate of success from indiscriminant DNA testing of large numbers of cases is likely to be well below 50 percent. Finally, the first type, or classic, cold-case investigation is likely to incur the highest costs and to have a low rate of success, even if judged by the lenient standard of exceptional clearances. Assessments of the value of cold cases need to draw these distinctions when estimating the value of investments made in resources to investigate cold cases.

We also note that some of our findings echo those of a mid-1970s RAND study of investigations (Greenwood, Chaiken, and Petersilia, 1977). Like the authors of the earlier RAND work, we found that systems that monitor investigations and investigator actions are either weak or nonexistent. Both the earlier study and our study also found that investigators were oriented toward clearing cases rather than winning convictions in court. These similarities after 35 years are striking.

Finally, we want to reiterate potential problems with both the survey and case-file study samples that could limit our findings. The survey response rate was low. We do not know whether this reflects apathy or confusion on the part of the agencies that received the survey or whether agencies that placed little or no emphasis on cold-case investigations simply did not see a reason to return a survey that dealt with how cold-case investigations were conducted. The three homicide sites that we selected for case-file work were chosen for reasons of convenience, access, and feasibility rather than being chosen randomly from among the 12 agencies we identified from our Internet survey. We do not know whether findings from these sites are representative of agencies that conduct a high volume of cold-case investigations.

Recommendations Going Forward

We come away from our investigation having more questions than answers about cold-case investigations. We were surprised at the lack of accountability in cold-case work. What is the main purpose of investing resources in cold-case investigations? Is it simply to respond to a victim's family's concerns that justice be done? That is highly satisfying to the individuals who work on cold cases, but it is not a good organizational rationale for investing time and money in an investigation. Is the purpose to increase clearance rates? To an extent, this does seem to be the rationale for working on cold cases. The more cold cases solved within a reporting period, the higher the period's overall homicide clearance rate.

But the primary justification for working cold cases has to be the same as the reason for working new cases: to bring perpetrators to justice and protect society from dangerous individuals. If that is the purpose of working cold cases, then the bottom line must be not just whether a case is cleared but whether a perpetrator is arrested, tried, and convicted.

Yet, we were surprised to learn that there is little emphasis on convictions as a goal of cold-case investigations and little tracking of conviction rates for cold cases. If obtaining a conviction is the ultimate goal, then it would seem logical for cold-case investigators to work closely with prosecutors when screening cases so they could decide whether, if the case were to be solved, there would likely be a prosecutable case. This is the model that was being used in the Denver site for the sexual-assault cold-case project. Police investigators sat down with prosecutors to determine whether each case that had material that could be submitted for DNA testing was likely to result in a conviction, assuming that a CODIS hit would be made on suspect DNA.

We did not see evidence that cold-case units were tracking conviction rates or other basic information on the efficacy and efficiency of cold-case investigations. Agencies had basic statistics on the number of cold cases worked, the number cleared by arrest, and the number of exceptional clearances. But they did not generally have information on court filings, convictions, sentences, or the time spent on cold-case investigations relative to the number of clearances obtained. In agencies where there are a fixed number of dedicated cold-case investigators, it is relatively straightforward to divide the hours worked by number of cases cleared. However, we observed that the number of cold-case investigators is not always fixed and that detectives switch back and forth between active and cold-case investigations.

After reviewing these results, we suggest two topics that should be researched to better understand the potential for cold-case investigations.

Conduct a Cost-Effectiveness Analysis of Investigator Time Spent on Cold Cases Versus New Cases

Because of the paucity of data on cold-case investigations, we know little about the return on investment of investigative resources put into cold cases relative to active cases. For a police agency with a fixed investigation budget, the question of what proportion of resources should be diverted to cold cases is a practical decision with important consequences. Collecting information in multiple selected agencies would help inform those decisions:

- Assemble statistics on the number of cases investigated, cases cleared, and arrests made for cold-case versus new investigations. This information could be gathered in compiled form from quarterly or annual reports, to the extent that it is available. However, because we have found that compiled information is especially scarce for cold-case investigations, we anticipate that, often, this information would have to be compiled from unit logs or the logs of individual investigators.
- Develop estimates of time spent on cold-case and active-case investigations by coding the frequency of different types of investigative activities (e.g., interviewing witnesses, querying investigative databases, preparing evidence for forensic testing, administrative tasks) on active and cold cases. One way to do this is to interview investigators to determine the average time involved for each type of investigative activity. Combining these two sources of information (activity frequency and time estimates from interviews) would allow for the development of estimates of average investigative times for active and cold cases.

Using the data collected, it would be possible to develop cost-effectiveness models that relate the average amount of time spent on active and cold-case investigations to clearances and arrests. The models would specify the expected number of clearances and arrests per hour of effort expended on active case and cold-case investigations.

Assess the Conviction Rate for Cold Cases, and Determine Whether Involvement of Prosecutors in Investigations Leads to a Higher Rate of Convictions

In a sample of agencies that conduct a large number of cold-case investigations, one could determine the conviction rate for successful cold-case investigations (i.e., those investigations that resulted in a clearance), what proportion of cleared cases are filed, and what proportion of the filings result in convictions. It would also be useful to collect reasons prosecutors gave for not filing cases and reasons for dismissal stated in prosecutor files for those cases that were filed but later dismissed. Interviews with detectives and prosecutors would provide further insight into the most-common reasons that some cleared cold cases do not result in convictions.

Analysis of these data would yield some important pieces of information, including the following:

- the average rate of case filings and convictions
- comparison of filing and conviction rates across sites to determine whether sites where police cold-case investigators consult with prosecutors throughout the investigative process have a higher rate of filings and convictions than other jurisdictions
- statistical models that relate case characteristics to filings and convictions. This could result in recommendations about how cold-case investigations ought to be prioritized to maximize convictions.

Law Enforcement Cold-Case Survey Instrument

1. Agency name

2. Please indicate your position in the agency, your connection to the cold-case unit if you have one, and, if you are not in the cold-case unit, the unit to which you are attached:
   a. Administrator, cold-case investigations
   b. Administrator, general investigations
   c. Investigator, cold-case investigations
   d. Investigator, general investigations
   e. Other:

3. By what process does your agency formally close (or relegate to inactive status) those criminal investigations that have been actively investigated but remain unsolved with few or no workable leads?
   a. This agency has no such mechanism; all cases are officially open even with no active pursuit.
   b. Periodic review and decision by a committee of investigators and/or supervisors
   c. Individual review and decision by investigative supervisor(s)
   d. Case investigator makes the decision.
   e. Other mechanism (please describe):

4. As a general practice, how long do standard case investigations other than homicide remain open before being reviewed for closure or inactive status?
   a. No such practice; all cases remain open (check only if "a" was checked in question 3)
   b. No set time; decisions are case-specific
   c. Less than one month
   d. One month to three months
   e. More than three months but less than six months
   f. Six months to one year
   g. More than one year but subject to closing

5. As a general practice, how long do homicide cases remain open before being reviewed for closure or inactive status?
   a. No such practice; all cases remain open (check only if "a" was checked in question 3)
   b. No set time; decisions are case-specific
   c. Less than six months
   d. Less than one year
   e. More than three months but less than six months
   f. Six months to one year
   g. More than one year but subject to closing

6. A cold case is generally considered to be one that was actively investigated at the time of original report and was subsequently closed or suspended for lack of evidence to pursue the case further. How does your agency specifically define ?

7. Does your agency formally reactivate and investigate cold cases?
   a. Yes
   b. No

8. Does your agency employ a formal protocol to determine selection and prioritization of cases for reinvestigation?
   a. Yes
   b. No

9. Which of the following are elements of the cold-case protocol? (Check all that apply.)
   - Age of case
   - Systematic reexamination of open cases
   - Availability of new material for DNA testing
   - Availability of other new physical evidence
   - Misplaced evidence discovered
   - New technology available for DNA testing old evidence
   - New technology available for other physical evidence
   - New witnesses come forward
   - Witnesses recant previous statements
   - Recovered memory
   - Prior conviction overturned
   - Other:

10. Please indicate the total number of cold cases actively investigated by your agency in the past year in the following categories (if the number is an estimate, please indicate by placing an "E" next to the entry).

Crime	Cold Cases Actively Worked in Past Year	Cold Cases Cleared in Past Year
Homicide and manslaughter		
Sex offenses (forcible rape or sodomy, sexual assault with an object, forcible fondling)		
Kidnapping/abduction		
Arson		
Robbery		
Burglary		
Embezzlement/fraud		
Missing persons		
Total		

11. Which of the following best describes your agency's cold-case investigation structure? Check all that apply.
   - Formal cold-case squad/unit
   - Designated cold-case investigator
   - Case is reassigned to the original lead
   - Case is assigned as part of the regular workload
   - Other (please explain):

12. Regardless of whether your department has a specialized cold-case unit, please estimate the number of full-time equivalents (FTE) assigned to work on cold cases (count staff who work on cold cases part time as fractions of FTEs):
   a. number of sworn FTEs:
   b. number of civilian FTEs:

13. Please estimate the caseload (those cases actively worked at any given time) of investigators assigned to cold cases:

14. Please estimate the proportion of cold-case investigations in which a perpetrator was identified have resulted in
   a. arrest:
   b. conviction:

15. What criteria do your agency use to evaluate the effectiveness of cold-case investigations?

Funding for Cold Cases

16. What is the nature of the funding for your agency's cold-case unit?
   - Established line item in the agency budget
   - Entirely grant funded
   - Funded by a combination of grant or private endowment seed money and supplemental agency budget money
   - Other (please explain):

17. If your agency's cold-case investigations are entirely grant funded, which of the following apply?
   - Agency/civil jurisdiction has committed itself to continuing the costs of cold-case work as a new budget line or within the existing budget structure
   - Plans for continuing cold-case investigations as part of the agency budget are under way or under discussion
   - Cold-case investigations will cease with the expiration of external funding
   - Other (please specify):

18. Does your agency receive funding from the U.S. Department of Justice specifically for cold-case investigation?
   a. Yes
   b. No

19. What was the total level of funding (all sources) for cold-case investigations within your agency for the past budget year? ($)

20. Please indicate the amount of funding provided annually for cold-case investigation by each of the following (if applicable):
   - Agency standard budget ($)
   - Agency supplemental budget ($)
   - Federal support (e.g., grants) ($)
   - Private foundation/donations ($)
   - Other sources ($)

DNA Evidence

21. How many DNA samples from cold cases were submitted to labs for testing in the past year?
   - Exact number or
   - Estimated

22. How many of the DNA samples submitted resulted in matches that identified a known suspect?
   - Exact number or
   - Estimated

23. How many of the DNA samples submitted resulted in matches that linked the case to an as-yet-unknown suspect in other investigations?
   - Exact number or
   - Estimated (estimate only if the exact number is not documented)

24. Does your agency have specific policies on the types of cold cases or circumstances under which DNA samples are submitted for matching?
   a. Yes
   b. No (If the answer is "no," skip to question 25.)

24a. If "yes," please describe:

Factors Promoting Cold-Case Solvability

25. Which of the following forms of institutional support does the agency provide to cold-case investigators?
   - Take-home cars assigned to individuals who investigate cold cases
   - Allow investigators to receive overtime pay without supervisory approval
   - Allow investigators to receive overtime pay with supervisory approval
   - Funding available to travel to other jurisdictions to pursue leads
   - Incentives to work on cold cases (If no incentive is given, skip to question 26.)

25A. What types of incentives are used?
   - Promotion
   - Promotability factor
   - Pay bonuses
   - Choice of shifts
   - Flexible hours
   - Choice of next assignment
   - Extra training
   - Other (please specify)

26. Which of the following elements are employed by your agency as part of its strategy for pursuing cold cases (check all that apply)?
   - Assign senior/experienced investigators
   - Assign teams of investigators to cold cases
   - Require specialized training in cold-case investigation
   - Specialized cold-case training available on a voluntary basis
   - Maintain a cold-case database
   - Active participation in information-sharing systems (e.g., RISS, LEO)
   - Formal coordination, consultation with state
   - Formal coordination, consultation with federal agencies
   - Formal media liaison

27. Please rate the factors below on a scale of 1 to 5 in terms of (a) how important that factor is in your agency's decision to actively investigate a cold case and (b) how important you believe it is for cold-case solvability (1 = contributes little or nothing, 5 = contributes a great deal):

Factor	Rating of Importance for Deciding to Actively Work Cold Cases (1–5)	Rating of Importance for Solving Cold Cases (1–5)
(1) Queries from family members or victim		
(2) Media attention paid to case		
(3) New witness information provided		
(3) Other new information provided by citizens or informants		
(4) Availability of outstanding leads to pursue		
(5) Potential of obtaining additional information from witnesses		
(6) Availability of DNA evidence that could be submitted for CODIS or other database match		
(7) Availability of fingerprint evidence of IAFIS quality		
(8) Murder weapon recovered		
(9) Projectiles/casings recovered of quality to submit for database match		
(10) Availability of other physical evidence (specify type(s)		
(11) Case fits pattern of serial crimes		
(12) Statute of limitations about to expire		
(13) Case age		
(14) Aggravating circumstances (innocence of victim, hate crime, heinousness of crime)		
(15) Evidence has been properly handled and stored over the course of the investigation		
(16) Case file is complete and retrievable		
(17) Original investigators/responding officers are available for interview		
(18) Original investigator case notes are available		
(19) Victim has been identified		
(20) Suspect has been identified		

APPENDIX B

Cold-Case Data Abstraction Form, Baltimore Example

Case ID

Coder

Case Status

Part I: Answer the questions in this part based on information determined during the initial investigation only.

For each item, circle the appropriate response option:

1. Victim information
   Name
   a. Race: Black, White, Hispanic, Asian, Other, Unknown
   b. Gender: M F
   c. Age
   d. Gang member: Y N Unknown
   e. Drug dealer: Y N
   f. Illegal immigrant: Y N Unknown
   g. Drug user: Y N Unknown
   h. Prostitution: Y N Unknown

2. Crime context
   a. Location of body: Residential building, Other indoor space, Car, Private outdoor space, Public outdoor space, Other, Unknown
   b. Time between death and recovery of body

3. Contact between victim and perpetrator
   a. Struggle preceded death: Y N Unknown
   b. Method of death: Shot, Stabbed, Strangled, Bludgeoned, Smothered, Beating, Other, Unknown

4. Motivation/cause (circle all that apply)
   a. Motivation known: Y N Unknown
   b. Drug feud/rivalry: Very likely, Likely, Unlikely
   c. Theft/robbery: Very likely, Likely, Unlikely

d. Personal/emotional (e.g., retaliation, argument): Very likely, Likely, Unlikely
e. Gang rivalry: Very likely, Likely, Unlikely
f. Sexual assault: Very likely, Likely, Unlikely
g. Accidental (victim not intended target): Very likely, Likely, Unlikely
h. Random (general retaliation against society or subgroup): Very likely, Likely, Unlikely

5. Key person of interest
   a. Primary suspect identified? Y N
      - If yes, how:
      - If yes, interviewed? Y N Unknown
      - If yes, arrested? Y N Unknown; If not arrested, why not?
   b. If no primary suspect, are there key persons of interest identified by name? Y N
      - If yes, how:

6. Witnesses
   a. Have eyewitnesses been identified? Y N
      - If yes: Were witnesses available to interview? Y N Unknown Not applicable
      - If yes: Were witnesses able to give a description of the perpetrator? Y N Unknown Not applicable
      - If yes: Were witnesses able to provide the identity of the perpetrator? Y N Unknown Not applicable
   b. Other witnesses or informants? Y N Unknown
      - If yes: Were witnesses able to give a description of the perpetrator? Y N Unknown Not applicable
      - If yes: Were witnesses able to provide the identity of the perpetrator? Y N Unknown Not applicable

7. Weapon evidence
   a. Murder weapon recovered? Y N Unknown Not applicable
   b. If firearm, were shell casings recovered? Y N Unknown Not applicable
   c. If firearm, were slugs recovered? Y N Unknown Not applicable

8. Suspect fingerprint evidence
   a. Prints recovered? Y N Unknown Not applicable
   b. Identification made? Y N Unknown Not applicable

9. DNA evidence
   a. Potential suspect DNA evidence recovered? Y N Unknown Not applicable
   b. Suspect identified through DNA testing? Y N Unknown Not applicable
   c. Match made to other crime scene? Y N Unknown Not applicable

Part II: Answer the questions in this part based on the cold-case investigative process.

1. Age of the case at the time the cold-case investigation was opened? (months)
2. Basis for opening a cold-case investigation? (circle as many as apply)
   a. Routine, based on elapsed time since original investigation

b. Family inquiry into status of case
c. Media inquiry into case
d. New physical information became available
e. Availability of new methods to test existing evidence
f. New information from witnesses
g. Confession/statements of perpetrator
h. Other:
i. Unknown

3. Actions taken by cold-case investigators? (circle all that apply)
   a. Tested/retested physical evidence
   b. Reinterviewed previous witnesses or suspects
   c. Interviewed new witnesses or suspects
   d. Developed new theory of motivation or new suspect
   e. Pursued outstanding leads
   f. Entered into investigative database (e.g., VICAP)
   g. Conducted additional witness interviews
   h. Wrote routine summary and updated computer database
   i. Background criminal checks of the suspects
   j. No evidence of any further actions taken
   k. Photo or lineup identification attempted
   l. Unknown

4. Final status: (circle one only)
   a. Cleared by arrest
   b. Exceptional clearance: Why? (check one only)
      – Suspect unavailable, incarcerated
      – Suspect unavailable, deceased
      – Insufficient evidence to arrest
      – Other:
   c. Not resolved

If case was solved, what were most important factors in reaching a conclusion?

References

Addington, Lynn A., "Using National Incident-Based Reporting System Murder Data to Evaluate Clearance Predictors: A Research Note," *Homicide Studies*, Vol. 10, No. 2, May 2006, pp. 140–152.

Ahlberg, J., and J. Knutsson, *Why Do Clearance Rates Vary?* Stockholm, Sweden: National Council for Crime Prevention, 1987.

Alderden, Megan A., and Timothy A. Lavery, "Predicting Homicide Clearances in Chicago: Investigating Disparities in Predictors Across Different Types of Homicide," *Homicide Studies*, Vol. 11, No. 2, May 2007, pp. 115–132.

Baskin, Deborah, and Ira Sommers, "The Influence of Forensic Evidence on the Case Outcome of Homicide Incidents," *Journal of Criminal Justice*, Vol. 38, No. 46, November–December 2010, pp. 1141–1149.

Bloch, Peter B., and James Bell, *Managing Investigations: The Rochester System*, Washington, D.C.: Police Foundation, 1976.

Borg, Marian J., and Karen F. Parker, "Mobilizing Law in Urban Areas: The Social Structure of Homicide Clearance Rates," *Law and Society Review*, Vol. 35, No. 2, 2001, pp. 435–466.

Burrows, John, and Roger Tarling, *Clearing Up Crime*, London, UK: Her Majesty's Stationery Office, 1982.

Campbell Collaboration, "Guidelines for Preparation of Review Protocols," January 1, 2001. As of September 19, 2011:
http://www.campbellcollaboration.org/artman2/uploads/1/C2_Protocols_guidelines_v1.pdf

Cardarelli, A., and D. Cavanaugh, *Uncleared Homicides in the United States: An Exploratory Study of Trends and Patterns*, paper presented at the annual meeting of the American Society of Criminology, 1992.

Chaiken, Jan M., Peter W. Greenwood, and Joan R. Petersilia, *The Criminal Investigation Process: A Summary Report*, Santa Monica, Calif.: RAND Corporation, P-5628-1, 1976. As of September 19, 2011:
http://www.rand.org/pubs/papers/P5628-1.html

Cordner, Gary W., "Police Agency Size and Investigative Effectiveness," *Journal of Criminal Justice*, Vol. 17, No. 3, 1989, pp. 145–155.

Davies, Heather J., *Understanding Variations in Murder Clearance Rates: The Influence of the Political Environment*, Washington, D.C.: American University, doctoral dissertation, May 2004.

———, "Understanding Variations in Murder Clearance Rates: The Influence of the Political Environment," *Homicide Studies*, Vol. 11, No. 2, May 2007, pp. 133–150.

Eck, John E., *Managing Case Assignments: The Burglary Investigation Decision Model Replication*, Washington, D.C.: Police Executive Research Forum, 1979.

———, *Solving Crimes: The Investigation of Burglary and Robbery*, Washington, D.C.: Police Executive Research Forum, 1983.

———, "Criminal Investigation," in Gary W. Cordner and Donna C. Hale, eds., *What Works in Policing? Operations and Administration Examined*, Cincinnati, Ohio: Anderson Publishing Company, 1992, pp. 19–34.

Elliott, J. F., "Crime Control Teams: An Alternative to the Conventional Operational Procedure of Investigating Crimes," *Journal of Criminal Justice*, Vol. 6, No. 1, Spring 1978, pp. 11–23.

Federal Bureau of Investigation, *Crime in the United States: The Uniform Crime Report—1963*, Washington, D.C., July 1964.

———, *Crime in the United States: 1997 Uniform Crime Reports*, Washington, D.C., November 22, 1998. As of September 19, 2011:
http://www.fbi.gov/about-us/cjis/ucr/crime-in-the-u.s/1997/toc97.pdf

Federal Judicial Center, *Reference Manual on Scientific Evidence*, 2nd ed., Washington, D.C., 2000. As of September 19, 2011:
http://purl.access.gpo.gov/GPO/LPS19667

Forst, Brian, F. J. Leahy, J. Shirhall, and J. Bartolomeo, *Arrest Convictability as a Measure of Police Performance*, Washington, D.C.: National Institute of Justice, July 1982.

Fyfe, James J., John S. Goldcamp, and Michael D. White, *Strategies for Reducing Homicide: The Comprehensive Homicide Initiative in Richmond, California*, Washington, D.C.: Bureau of Justice Assistance, December 1997.

Gans, Jeremy, and Gregor Urbas, *DNA Identification in the Criminal Justice System*, Canberra, A.C.T.: Australian Institute of Criminology, May 2002.

Gay, William G., H. Talmadge Day, and Jane P. Woodward, *Neighborhood Team Policing*, Washington, D.C.: National Institute of Law Enforcement and Criminal Justice, Law Enforcement Assistance Administration, U.S. Department of Justice, February 1977.

Geberth, Vernon J., *Practical Homicide Investigation: Tactics, Procedures, and Forensic Techniques*, 3rd ed., Boca Raton, Fla.: CRC Press, 1996.

Gilbert, James N., "A Study of the Increased Rate of Unsolved Criminal Homicide in San Diego, California and Its Relationship to Police Investigative Effectiveness," *American Journal of Police*, Vol. 2, No. 2, 1983, pp. 149–166.

Golding, Jonathan M., Terri L. Stewart, John A. Yozwiak, Yas Djadali, and Rebecca Polley Sanchez, "Impact of DNA Evidence in a Child Sexual Assault Trial," *Child Maltreatment*, Vol. 5, No. 4, November 2000, pp. 373–383.

Goulka, Jeremiah, Carl F. Matthies, Emma Disley, and Paul Steinberg, *Toward a Comparison of DNA Profiling and Databases in the United States and England*, Santa Monica, Calif.: RAND Corporation, TR-918-ISEC, 2010. As of September 19, 2011:
http://www.rand.org/pubs/technical_reports/TR918.html

Greenwood, Peter W., Jan M. Chaiken, and Joan Petersilia, *The Criminal Investigation Process*, Lexington, Mass.: D. C. Heath, 1977.

Greenwood, Peter W., and Joan R. Petersilia, *The Criminal Investigation Process*, Vol. I: *Summary and Policy Implications*, Santa Monica, Calif.: RAND Corporation, R-1776-DOJ, 1975. As of September 19, 2011:
http://www.rand.org/pubs/reports/R1776.html

Hickman, Matthew J., and Brian A. Reaves, *Local Police Departments, 2000: Law Enforcement Management and Administrative Statistics*, Washington, D.C.: Bureau of Justice Statistics, NCJ 196002, 2003.

Hillen, B. F., "New York City Police Department's Investigative Case Management System: An Impact Study," *Journal of Police Science and Administration*, Vol. 7, No. 4, December 1979, pp. 400–425.

Horvath, F., and R. Meesig, "A Content Analysis of Textbooks on Criminal Investigation: An Evaluative Comparison to Empirical Research Findings on the Investigative Process and the Role of Forensic Evidence," *Journal of Forensic Science*, Vol. 43, No. 1, January 1998, pp. 133–140.

Hsu, Ko-Hsin, *Homicide Clearance Determinants: An Analysis of the Police Departments of the 100 Largest U.S. Cities*, College Park, Md.: University of Maryland, master's thesis, 2007. As of September 19, 2011:
http://hdl.handle.net/1903/7391

IACP—*See* International Association of Chiefs of Police.

International Association of Chiefs of Police, *Murder in America: Recommendations from the IACP Murder Summit*, Alexandria, Va., May 1995.

Jensen, Carl Julius, *A Test of Bounded Rationality on Police Investigative Decision Making*, College Park, Md.: University of Maryland, thesis, 2003.

Keel, Timothy G., John P. Jarvis, and Yvonne E. Muirhead, "An Exploratory Analysis of Factors Affecting Homicide Investigations," *Homicide Studies*, Vol. 13, No. 1, 2009, pp. 50–68.

Kennedy, David, "Pulling Levers: Getting Deterrence Right," *National Institute of Justice Journal*, Vol. 236, July 1998, pp. 2–8. As of September 19, 2011:
https://www.ncjrs.gov/pdffiles/jr000236.pdf

Lee, Catherine, "The Value of Life in Death: Multiple Regression and Event History Analyses of Homicide Clearance in Los Angeles County," *Journal of Criminal Justice*, Vol. 33, No. 6, November–December 2005, pp. 527–534.

Litwin, Kenneth J., "A Multilevel Multivariate Analysis of Factors Affecting Homicide Clearances," *Journal of Research in Crime and Delinquency*, Vol. 41, No. 4, November 2004, pp. 327–351.

Litwin, Kenneth J., and Yili Xu, "The Dynamic Nature of Homicide Clearances: A Multilevel Model Comparison of Three Time Periods," *Homicide Studies*, Vol. 11, No. 2, May 2007, pp. 94–114.

Lovrich, Nicholas P., Travis C. Pratt, Michael J. Gaffney, Charles L. Johnson, Christopher H. Asplen, Lisa H. Hurst, and Timothy M. Schellberg, *National Forensic DNA Study Report, Final Report*, Pullman, Wash.: Division of Governmental Studies, Washington State University, February 2004. As of September 19, 2011:
https://www.ncjrs.gov/pdffiles1/nij/grants/203970.pdf

Maryland Public Information Act—*See* Maryland State Government Code Annotated, Section 10-612.

Maryland State Government Code Annotated, Title 10, Government procedures, Subtitle 6, Records, Part III, Access to public records.

McDowall, David, "Firearm Availability and Homicide Rates in Detroit, 1951–1986," *Social Forces*, Vol. 69, No. 4, June 1991, pp. 1085–1101.

McEwen, Tom, *Volume 1 Evaluation of the Phoenix Homicide Project: Final Report*, Washington, D.C.: National Institute of Justice, Office of Justice Programs, U.S. Department of Justice, July 2009.

Mouzos, Jenny, and Damon Muller, *Solvability Factors of Homicide in Australia: An Exploratory Analysis*, Canberra, A.C.T.: Australian Institute of Criminology, 2001.

National Institute of Justice, *A Study of Homicide in Eight U.S. Cities: An NIJ Intramural Research Project*, Washington, D.C., 1997. As of September 19, 2011:
http://purl.access.gpo.gov/GPO/LPS501

———, *Using DNA to Solve Cold Cases*, Washington, D.C., NCJ 194197, July 2002. As of September 19, 2011:
http://purl.access.gpo.gov/GPO/LPS27455

———, *Report to the Attorney General on Delays in Forensic DNA Analysis*, March 2003. As of September 19, 2011:
http://purl.access.gpo.gov/GPO/LPS42389

———, *DNA in "Minor" Crimes Yields Major Benefits in Public Safety*, November 2004. As of September 19, 2011:
http://purl.access.gpo.gov/GPO/LPS57433

NIJ—*See* National Institute of Justice.

Ousey, Graham C., and Matthew R. Lee, "To Know the Unknown: The Decline in Homicide Clearance Rates, 1980–2000," *Criminal Justice Review*, Vol. 35, No. 2, June 2010, pp. 141–158.

Paré, Paul-Philippe, Richard B. Felson, and Marc Ouimet, "Community Variation in Crime Clearance: A Multilevel Analysis with Comments on Assessing Police Performance," *Journal of Quantitative Criminology*, Vol. 23, No. 3, September 2007, pp. 243–258.

Parker, L., "Unsolved Killings on the Rise: Percent of Cases Closed Drops from 86% to 69%," *USA Today*, February 22, 2000, p. 01A.

Puckett, Janice L., and Richard J. Lundman, "Factors Affecting Homicide Clearances: Multivariate Analysis of a More Complete Conceptual Framework," *Journal of Research in Crime and Delinquency*, Vol. 40, No. 2, May 2003, pp. 171–193.

Regini, Charles L., "The Cold Case Concept." *FBI Law Enforcement Bulletin*, August 1997, pp. 1–6. As of September 19, 2011:
http://www2.fbi.gov/publications/leb/1997/aug971.htm

Regoeczi, Wendy C., John Jarvis, and Marc Riedel, "Clearing Murders: Is It About Time?" *Journal of Research in Crime and Delinquency*, Vol. 45, No. 2, May 2008, pp. 142–162.

Regoeczi, Wendy C., Leslie W. Kennedy, and Robert A. Silverman, "Uncleared Homicides: A Canada/United States Comparison," *Homicide Studies*, Vol. 4, No. 2, May 2000, pp. 135–161.

Richardson, Deborah A., and Rachel Kosa, *An Examination of Homicide Clearance Rates: Foundation for the Development of a Homicide Clearance Model*, Washington, D.C.: Police Executive Research Forum, 2001. As of September 19, 2011:
http://www.policeforum.org/library/homicide/Homicide%20Clearance%20Rates%20-%20Model.pdf

Riedel, Marc, *Stranger Violence: A Theoretical Inquiry*, New York: Garland Publishing, 1993.

———, *Violence, Homicides, and Clearances: Third Parties as Informants*, unpublished, 1994.

———, "Getting Away with Murder: An Examination of Arrest Clearances," in Carolyn Block and Richard Block, eds., *Trends, Risks, and Interventions in Lethal Violence: Proceedings of the Third Annual Spring Symposium of the Homicide Research Working Group*, Washington, D.C.: U.S. Department of Justice, National Institute of Justice, 1995a, pp. 91–98.

———, *Questions and Answers About Murder*, New York: McGraw-Hill, 1995b

———, "Arrest Clearances for Homicide: A Study of Los Angeles," in Robert A. Silverman, T. P. Thornberry, B. Cohen, and B. Krisberg, eds., *Crime and Justice at the Millennium: Essays by and in Honor of Marvin E. Wolfgang*, Boston, Mass.: Kluwer Academic, 2002, pp. 99–119.

Riedel, Marc, and John Jarvis, "The Decline of Arrest Clearances for Criminal Homicide: Causes, Correlates, and Third Parties," *Criminal Justice Policy Review*, Vol. 9, No. 3–4, 1999, pp. 279–306.

Riedel, Marc, and T. A. Rinehart, *Clearance, Missing Data, and Murder*, presented at the Annual Meeting of the Academy of Criminal Justice Sciences, Chicago, Ill., 1994.

———, "Murder Clearances and Missing Data," *Journal of Crime and Justice*, Vol. 19, No. 2, 1996, pp. 83–102.

Rinehart, T. A., *An Analysis of Police Clearances in Chicago: 1981–1991*, unpublished thesis, 1994.

Rojek, Dean G., "Changing Homicide Patterns," in Pamela K. Lattimore and Cynthia A. Nahabedian, eds., *The Nature of Homicide: Trends and Changes—Proceedings of the 1996 Meeting of the Homicide Research Working Group*, Santa Monica, Calif., c. 1996, pp. 106–125. As of September 19, 2011:
https://www.ncjrs.gov/pdffiles1/nij/166149.pdf

Sanders, William B., *Detective Work: A Study of Criminal Investigations*, New York: Free Press, 1977.

Schroeder, David A., and Michael D. White, "Exploring the Use of DNA Evidence in Homicide Investigations: Implications for Detective Work and Case Clearance," *Police Quarterly*, Vol. 12, No. 3, September 2009, pp. 319–342.

Schwartz, Alfred I., and Sumner N. Clarren, *The Cincinnati Team Policing Experiment: A Summary Report*, Washington, D.C.: Police Foundation, 1977.

Sherman, Lawrence W., "Evidence-Based Policing," *Ideas in American Policing*, July 1998. As of September 5, 2002:
http://www.policefoundation.org/pdf/Sherman.pdf

Skolnick, Jerome H., *Justice Without Trial: Law Enforcement in Democratic Society*, New York: Wiley, 1966.

Thompson, Cheryl W., "Families of Victims Often Left Wondering," *Washington Post*, December 4, 2000, p. A15. As of September 19, 2011:
http://www.washingtonpost.com/wp-dyn/content/article/2008/01/09/AR2008010902336.html

Thompson, Cheryl W., Ira Chinoy, and Barbara Vobejda, "Unsolved Killings Plague District," *Washington Post*, December 3, 2000, p. A01. As of September 19, 2011:
http://www.washingtonpost.com/wp-dyn/content/article/2008/01/09/AR2008010902327.html

Turner, Ryan, and Rachel Kosa, *Cold Case Squads: Leaving No Stone Unturned*, Washington, D.C.: Bureau of Justice Assistance, 2003.

U.S. House of Representatives, Committee on the Judiciary, Subcommittee on Crime, Terrorism, and Homeland Security, *Advancing Justice Through Forensic DNA Technology: Hearing Before the Subcommittee on Crime, Terrorism, and Homeland Security of the Committee on the Judiciary, House of Representatives, One Hundred Eighth Congress, First Session, July 17, 2003*, Washington, D.C., 2003. As of September 19, 2011:
http://purl.access.gpo.gov/GPO/LPS41128

Vobejda, Barbara, and Ira Chinoy, "As D.C. Police Falter, Revenge Fills the Void," *Washington Post*, December 5, 2000, p. A01. As of September 19, 2011:
http://www.washingtonpost.com/wp-dyn/content/article/2008/01/09/AR2008010902954.html

Weisheit, Ralph A., and L. Edward Wells, "Deadly Violence in the Heartland: Comparing Homicide Patterns in Nonmetropolitan and Metropolitan Counties," *Homicide Studies*, Vol. 9, No. 1, February 2005, pp. 55–80.

Wellford, Charles, James Cronin, Steve Brandl, Timothy Bynum, Tom Eversen, and Steve Galeria, *An Analysis of Variables Affecting the Clearance of Homicides: A Multistate Study*, Washington, D.C.: Justice Research and Statistics Association, October 1999. As of September 19, 2011:
http://www.jrsa.org/pubs/reports/Clearance_of_Homicide.html

Willman, Mark T., and John R. Snortum, "Detective Work: The Criminal Investigation Process in a Medium-Size Police Department," *Criminal Justice Review*, Vol. 9, No. 1, Spring 1984, pp. 33–39.

Willmer, M. A. P., *Crime and Information Theory*, Edinburgh, Scotland: University Press, 1970.

Xu, Yili, "Characteristics of Homicide Events and the Decline in Homicide Clearance: A Longitudinal Approach to the Dynamic Relationship, Chicago 1966–1995," *Criminal Justice Review*, Vol. 33, No. 4, December 2008, pp. 452–479.

Ybarrondo, P., "How Homicide Cases Are Really Handled," *Law Enforcement Quarterly*, May–July 1992, pp. 15–19, 25.

Young, Ayah, "Deadly Silence: Stop Snitching's Fatal Legacy," *Wiretap*, March 28, 2008. As of September 21, 2011:
http://www.wiretapmag.org/race/43473/